Dancing in Gumboots

Caitlin Press Inc.
8100 Alderwood Road, Halfmoon Bay, BC V0N 1Y1
www.caitlin-press.com

Text design and cover design by Vici Johnstone
Front cover photograph of Gloria Simpson and Jeanine Maars tree planting by Jane Gilchrist.
Back cover artwork by Lynda Glover

Printed in Canada

Caitlin Press Inc. acknowledges financial support from the Government of Canada and the Canada Council for the Arts, and the Province of British Columbia through the British Columbia Arts Council and the Book Publisher's Tax Credit.

Library and Archives Canada Cataloguing in Publication

Dancing in gumboots : adventure, love & resilience : women of the Comox Valley / Lou Allison and Jane Wilde, editors.

ISBN 978-1-987915-76-1 (softcover)

1. Women—British Columbia—Comox Valley—Biography. 2. Urban-rural migration—History—20th century. 3. Country life—British Columbia—Comox Valley. 4. Comox Valley (B.C.)—Biography. I. Allison, Lou, editor II. Wilde, Jane, 1955-, editor

HQ1459.B7D36 2018   305.409711'28   C2018-903395-9

Dancing in Gumboots

ADVENTURE, LOVE & RESILIENCE
WOMEN OF THE COMOX VALLEY

EDITED BY LOU ALLISON
WITH JANE WILDE

CAITLIN PRESS

We respectfully acknowledge
that we live, work and play
on the traditional lands of the
K'omoks First Nation.

Friends gather at the 1979 Comox Valley
Renaissance Fair.

Contents

Having traded her gumboots for moccasins, Roberta DeDoming is sockin' it to 'em on a Denman Island beach in 1975.

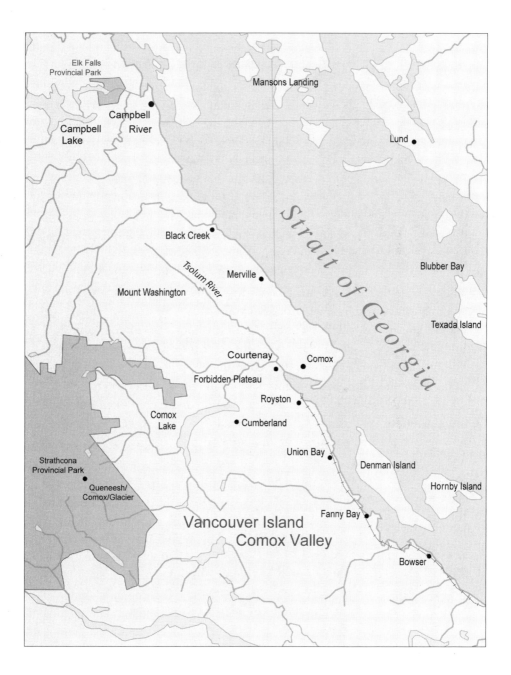

Editor's Note

Lou Allison

She did it again. My friend Jane Wilde is a force. In 2012 she inspired a group of writing neophytes to produce a book called *Gumboot Girls: Adventure, Love and Survival on British Columbia's North Coast*. The whole project, from beginning to end, was an adventure in itself. Six years later, the book quietly continues to roll along, garnering new readers and even critical attention from time to time.

After northern BC lost Jane to Vancouver Island in 2016, she called one day to ask: "Are you sitting down? I loved working on that project with you. Do you want to do it again? There are a lot of stories down here." I had thought the book was unrepeatable and, in many ways, it is. This new book, situated in the same time and demographic, is different. Many of the same themes emerged: hard work and parties, emancipation and commitment, motherhood and careers, self-discovery and self-sufficiency, and creating family and community. But there are also differences: many of these women are indelibly rooted in place, but also very well-travelled, spending time abroad, then and now. Their social and political activism, local and global, has created lasting legacies. Some founded businesses that evolved into local institutions. Most have stayed in the valley and surrounding islands and are deeply woven into the fabric of their chosen piece of paradise.

I am a northern girl, attuned to the rhythms of my chosen place, but I wonder where I would be if I had chosen to settle in the Comox Valley in 1974? I like to think that I would be friends with these marvellous women, part of the weft and warp of their caring community.

I feel honoured and privileged to be part of this project.

Introduction

JANE WILDE

It happened again. I recently moved to the Comox Valley, after living for forty years on the north coast of BC between Haida Gwaii and Prince Rupert, and I started to meet women from all over the world who had settled around the valley in the seventies. They seemed so familiar to me, and I wanted to know their stories.

The idea of saving women's stories from the seventies had evolved after I read Sheila Weller's *Girls Like Us: Carole King, Joni Mitchell, Carly Simon—and the Journey of a Generation*. I realized that she was also describing my story and that of many of my friends who grew up in the sixties and seventies. In communities around the world, young women were living the music Sheila described, experiencing the sexual revolution that changed relationship and marriage expectations, travelling and exploring rural lifestyles despite urban upbringings and trying non-traditional careers using new skills and strengths. Some American women moved to Canada to escape the impact of the Vietnam War on their lives. I realized it was important to capture the uniqueness of our shared experience exploring the world with freedom and opportunities that were new to women.

In 2011 I easily convinced thirty-four women friends to write their stories of coming to the north coast of BC in the seventies. My friend and neighbour Lou Allison agreed to be the editor, and we found an agreeable publisher, Muskeg Press. *Gumboot Girls: Adventure, Love and Survival on British Columbia's North Coast* was published in 2012. In late 2013, Muskeg Press folded and Caitlin Press took us aboard. Our collection of stories is a surprise bestseller that continues to resonate. People, especially women, find our stories engaging, entertaining and relatable.

In 2017, under the representation of Caitlin Press, it was again easy to find thirty-two women who came to the Comox Valley in the seventies and who were willing to share their stories and photos of that time. I am curating the photos, and Lou again agreed to be the editor. Together, the photos and stories show the fullness of these women's lives, similar in some respects but also significantly different to the *Gumboot Girls* experiences. There were different opportunities in the Comox Valley from those on the north coast. Reasonably priced acreages were available to buy. The weather was suitable for successful large-scale gardening, farming and self-sufficiency. Tree planting was a lucrative career option for many of the writers in those years. The larger Vancouver Island population and easy access to Vancouver and Victoria offered creative opportunities for careers as artists and musicians. The burgeoning Arts Alliance and the annual Renaissance Fair that became a destination event enticed many travellers to stay. Over forty years later, only three of the writers have moved away from the Comox Valley.

The writers in *Dancing in Gumboots* represent a small sampling of the thousands of young women who travelled to Vancouver Island in the seventies. Their stories provide a glimpse into the intensity of the times that Sheila Weller called "magical and transformative."

Hippies, Homesteads & Hubris

ROBERTA DeDOMING
Arrived in 1970

Already landowners, we arrived on the shores of Denman Island at apple blossom time in 1970, having bought our island property in 1968 from a member of one of the original homesteading families. Two of the three couples in our group of friends had driven across the continent from New York City with plenty of youthful enthusiasm, but not much of a plan, to find land in British Columbia. The late Wallace Baikie, from whom we bought our land, made us promise we weren't real estate speculators from New York before he agreed to sell us his 42.5-acre farm on Denman for the staggering price of ten thousand dollars. If there was anyone in the world who looked less like real estate moguls from New York, it was us. He requested and graciously accepted the ten-dollar down payment for his old family farm on Denman Island. We had secured our future home.

Now we just had to earn the money to pay for it. Back in the city, I earned my share by hack writing for movie magazines like *Screen Stars* and *Photoplay* at a hundred dollars per article, while my husband, Marc, left his job as a travel agent and worked in construction so he could learn some practical building skills.

When we were travelling back to New York via California, we had stopped in Berkeley and dropped in on Patti Willis and her then husband Manny, who were friends of a friend. We soon discovered that Manny and Stu, one of our Denman-bound group, had attended elementary school together in New York's Greenwich Village many years ago. Perhaps it was the instant camaraderie of this long-ago connection that encouraged us to lure them with apples we had sneaked across the border from Canada and tell them the tale of our recent adventure: "We just bought land on a magic island and we found some land for you too, by a beautiful lake. You should come. Find some friends and move to Denman Island." So they did.

I wish I still had that beloved alpaca poncho—and, while we're wishing, that head of hair!

Our group planned to leave the US for the usual reasons in the late sixties. The Vietnam War was raging and we were opposed to it. Our three men had gotten their draft deferments on dubious medical grounds. Mental illness? Rheumatic hearts? Some anti-war-prone MD friends were happy to oblige. We had protested with so many others and witnessed arrests and police violence, including attacks with billy clubs. A few of us had been arrested at a large demonstration in Greenwich Village. We thought, *Hell with this, let's go to Canada.* We wanted to settle in a country where English was spoken, where politics tended toward the progressive, where the weather was not too extreme and where we could look for property without the expense and complexity of leaving the continent. The West Coast of our northern neighbour Canada seemed to fit.

We did not have an articulated vision of the life we were going to live or how we would support ourselves, but were fuelled by a strong youthful inclination to venture forth and live more authentic and natural lives. We would build a single home to house all three families, and we would grow our own food and reinvent civilization. No big deal.

So, trading giant skyscrapers for giant cedars, we left Manhattan Island for a rural life on Denman Island, about the same size but with a population of just under three hundred.

When we arrived on Denman we were three couples, two of whom had small daughters. Our daughter, Eva, was a sixteen-month-old toddler, and tiny Allie was five months old. We lived in tents among the apple trees in our orchard for nearly half a year. When it rained, we stepped out of our beds and into our gumboots. First things first, the outhouse hole was dug. We set up a kitchen under the giant maple trees. Quite soon after our arrival, we designed and began building our Orchard House. When the house was completed, after the autumn rains had begun and my chilblains had set in, we all thankfully moved indoors.

We tried to make it work and we had our moments of communal warmth, but quirky personalities clashed, lifestyle differences grated and none of us had the communication skills to work things through. I cannot remember any satisfactory group conversations among us at that time. Outdoors there were puddles and indoors muddles, along with an unsatisfactory and murky atmosphere.

It wasn't too long before the couple who had the infant daughter, obviously stressed and needing their privacy, decided to build a cabin at the back of our property up on a ridge, a labour-intensive project. Their cabin was situated as far as it could possibly be from the original Orchard House.

By the close of 1973, two of the three couples had left Denman Island, the Ridge House family moving to Cumberland, where their second child was born. Now with a toddler themselves and realizing that country life was simply not for them, the other departing family left for Vancouver, where they live to this day. We are still very close friends, more like family. From our hopes for group living and working together, we had shrunk back down to conventional nuclear families. My husband, Marc, and I and our little girl, Eva, remained on Denman. Our son, Rama, was born in mid-1973.

When they reached school age, my two children attended the original two-room schoolhouse on our island, living happily without TV and with few peers. When Eva started school, there were seven school-age kids on the island. Our children picked berries, climbed trees and played with the cats, the chickens and the goats who occasionally jumped into the house through the dining room window, crashing around and delighting the kids no end.

During those early years, more expats moved to Denman Island, some living in converted goat barns and chicken coops, all with interesting stories to tell. There were artisans getting their potteries and workshops going, potluck dinners, work bees, dances and parties. There were pagan gatherings, the Renaissance Fairs on Vancouver Island, and Denman had a funky and fun summer theatre group called Manfrog's Circus. There was music-making, magic mushroom-taking, marijuana-growing, skinny-dipping at the lake, the dissolving of marriages, the celebrating of new ones and the additions of infants who grew like glorious weeds. As the population swelled, so did the rumours of sexual liaisons, some of which were even true. We lived with the comic irony of the old-timers expressing their outrage at our hippie ways of going on, as they dismissed their own suspiciously similar foibles and indulgences as being "not the same thing at all."

We dug clams and gathered oysters, the kids having a great time helping and splashing around in tide pools. In herring season we gathered at the edge of our island at Fillongley Park, scooped the tiny fish out of the water and made pickled herring. We picked wild berries and stalked wild asparagus. We kept chickens for eggs and meat, goats for milk and cheese, and eventually we had a horse.

We were surrounded by acres of Douglas fir, hemlock and cedar trees, with ground covers of moss and Oregon grape that we picked for making jelly. When the autumn rains came, we'd gather baskets full of chanterelles in our woods. One spring there was a bumper crop of morels that sprang up in the orchard: I felt like I'd discovered gold the day I found that substantial patch of miniature cathedrals with their Gothic windows. Deer wandered, eagles soared. Our old orchard produced apples and plums in plenty. There was an apple press we used across the road and a tofu shop (the best tofu ever). We gardened and preserved food. I cooked, cleaned, sewed and knit. We took care of our growing children and each other.

Following up one of our interests, Marc came up with the idea of starting Ganden Herb Farm, and together we founded and operated Bodhi Tea, an herbal tea business for which we grew herbs, germinated and tended in our greenhouse. We concocted recipes for tea blends that were unique and delicious, blending our own and purchased herbs. Would that we'd had the business know-how to have kept that venture going. But we didn't, and our business eventually folded, as did our marriage. Marc and I separated in 1980 when I was thirty-eight. I moved to the Ridge House, where I lived for a few years with no electricity, no car access and no running water, but a small cistern that gathered roof runoff. Back to basics: chop wood and carry water. The kids spent time with us both, traipsing through the meadow back and forth between our houses. After some bumps in the road for each of us, both Marc and I went on to establish successful long-term relationships with others that lasted, for me twenty-five years, until Gerry's sudden and

Marc and me transplanting seedlings in the greenhouse. This image originally appeared in an article written by Des Kennedy in *Harrowsmith* magazine about our Ganden Herb Farm and Bodhi Tea business. Photo Paul Bailey, 1979

untimely death in 2007, just two months after our move from Denman to Courtenay. Marc (a.k.a. Swann in the last decades of his life) passed away in 2016 after a long illness.

During those early Denman years, I also worked as a birthing coach and attendant (what is now called a doula). Perhaps those birthing books around the house had something to do with my daughter's chosen profession. She became a doctor, an obstetrician-gynecologist.

Also in that first decade, I did a couple of stints working at the Denman Store's café, cooking and waiting on tables. For many years I worked as a home support worker. After studying in Arizona at an intensive workshop, I worked with others guiding in-depth visualizations. I helped to initiate our island food co-op and a preschool where I worked with the children. I answered phones for the Comox Valley crisis line. I travelled to Vancouver Island regularly as a member of Co-Val Choristers and can recall a few harrowing trips in a tiny motorized rowboat during ferry stoppages to get to rehearsals, especially critical since I often had solo roles in upcoming productions. I also helped co-found the Denman Island choral group, Harmonia Mundi, and directed it for several years. I read and studied independently, fuelling my interest in poetry, Jungian psychology, mysticism, Buddhism, new-paradigm thought and the many spiritual paths of our world. I also wrote and had poetry and the occasional book review published in journals and periodicals. Subsequently, I published a book of my selected poems, *Singing the Hummingbirds North* (2001), and most recently a memoir, *Out of the Blue: Musings on Synchronicity* (2016).

Until Gerry and I left Denman to move to Courtenay in 2007, I had lived on the same piece of land for thirty-seven years. I had changed husbands and homes but kept the same two children and still enjoy the blessing of them in my life, along with the addition of two adored grandchildren. Blended into that are my partner Gerry's two sons, my stepsons, who loved their childhood visits to the wilds of Denman. As an adult, one of my stepsons has lived on Denman for many years.

Leaving New York City and moving to Denman Island was a tremendous adventure. During my early years on Denman, I made a few cherished friends and others who I might not see very often anymore but will feel deeply connected to for life. Many of the cultural values that were seeded in the sixties are still with me as I have seen North American society at large adopt, develop and own these progressive ideas. Even if we were naive and clumsy in our efforts, surely we were in the vanguard. I get defensive when people disparage the sixties "hippies" as merely frivolous and flaky, failing to acknowledge the tremendous contributions to society made by alternative culture individuals and groups: environmentalism and ecology, connection to the natural world, self-sufficiency, sustainable development, the anti-nuclear and peace movements, peaceful protest and civil rights activism, shifts in attitudes and practices around birth and death, animal rights, food awareness, feminism, gender expression and gay rights issues, race equality issues, openness to elemental and Eastern religions, mindfulness, meditation, the idea of being spiritual but not conventionally religious, learning about and honouring of Indigenous history and cultures, and many back-to-basics ideas of simplicity and healthy living.

I sometimes think of those old days on Denman, when the population was so small that everyone knew everyone. I remember participating with the choir in Christmas Eve services in the beautiful old Anglican Church at the top of the ferry hill. The newcomers and the old-timers all gathered together as we honoured and celebrated the birth of a spiritual avatar who understood the nature of love and forgiveness. I imagine myself singing "O Holy Night" in harmony with Patti Willis in a tiny church on an island in the middle of nowhere. The phrase "What's a nice Jewish girl like you doing in a place like this?" goes through my mind, and I reply, "Creating a crazy-quilt mosaic of a life that suits me just fine."

I am filled with gratitude for Denman Island, for those now gone and all who still journey on her, for this wonderful Comox Valley, her natural wonders and her people, Indigenous and those from away, and for the many blessings of Canada, our vast and varied country.

I have never regretted any of it, neither the adventure of homesteading on Denman as a young woman nor the change in my later years to a very different life here in Courtenay. How textured and colourful are the threads that others have woven and continue to weave into my tapestry. The wonder of being here at all, as one by one we age and take our leave, as friends and life partners pass away. Inevitably roads diverge, choices are made. We bid our goodbyes to the "woulda, shoulda, couldas," those roads not taken, and then we must say goodbye to each other and the sheer magnificence of it all.

Pies, Pottery & Peace

PATTI WILLIS
Arrived in 1970

Courtenay, British Columbia, 1970: Butter tarts from the tiny health food store on Fourth Street, death notices of local residents posted on the corner of England and Fifth, and the preponderance of British novels in the storefront public library on Sixth were unmistakable evidence that I was no longer in California.

With hair to my waist and draped in a floor-length East Indian bedspread skirt, I arrived on Denman Island to become a land partner with nine others on 160 acres of farm, forest and wetlands. It was a serendipitous move. My mate at the time and I had met a group of New Yorkers who had just bought property on the island. They came through Berkeley, where I had been radicalized by the Free Speech Movement and a degree in philosophy while protesting in the civil rights and anti-war movements. The New Yorkers carried a hefty duffle bag of crisp, ruby-red apples, which they had smuggled across the border. The apples were highly biblical; we bit into one and were seduced into visiting these people in their Denman Garden of Eden, and ultimately to becoming settlers ourselves.

We were never a commune per se; we all still had our own nests. We tried eating together, but the newborn vegetarians (like myself) and the carnivores could never really forge a workable détente. We established a communal garden, but too many of us failed to close the gate, and the crops were marauded by cattle, horses and deer, even though my nearest neighbour and I, both pregnant at the time, wove a macramé fence out of baling twine as reinforcement. When our babies were born, we deposited their soiled paper diapers along the fenceline, as rumour had it they would keep the animals at bay. We did manage to have a communal cow: first Bossy, then Pansy, and finally the sweet-tempered Clairwyn. The cows put up with multiple milkmaids and gents, and they produced bountiful milk and rich cream. I always sang African-American spirituals while milking. The generous cows taught me to put milk in my tea, the Canadian way. The *I Ching*, which we consulted many times in those early days, counselled, "Care of the cow brings good fortune."

Eventually, I lived alone in a small cabin on the land, painting a mural on its front door and learning country ways. I once baked a terrible pie in gratitude for a kind neighbouring farmer's helpfulness to us clueless city slickers. I coaxed the wood stove for hours with wet wood to produce an inedible pie of 100 percent stone-ground, whole-wheat flour, solidified buckwheat honey and undercooked apples. The farmer, gentleman that he was, returned my pie plate and extolled that it was the best pie he had ever eaten. I spent most of my days in the woods, learning the names of plants, brewing exotic teas from my foraging and finding myself in stunned wonder in a cathedral of giant firs.

My philosophy degree being unmarketable, I had the good fortune of having studied pottery on the side with the famous Peter Voulkos (who would roll over in his grave to see my work now—underglaze paintings of dragonflies, moths and flowers on porcelain). At that time living in a converted sheep barn, my new mate and I set up booths at every Renaissance Fair, from the first to the last.

With our little daughter still in pyjamas, we piled into our decrepit station wagon to catch the first ferry to Vancouver. We humbly peddled our work

Daughter Lily lived free-range. I still unearth her Lego, Barbie accessories and marbles in my garden. Photo John Harned

from shop to shop, participated in the early Circle Craft Christmas Markets at the Vancouver East Cultural Centre, and after a lunch at the Naam, made fly-pasts to our favourite spots for treats to take back to Denman. Though I thought to give up pottery when other concerns, such as peace, called my name, one of my mentors, physicist and Quaker Dr. Ursula Franklin, sagely advised: "Go ahead and commit to these dire issues, but keep your hands in the clay." Fifty years of being a potter have served me well. For the past twenty-five years, I have been an owner of the Denman Craft Shop, with a collective of nine skilled and endlessly good-natured women.

I was born in July 1945, steps away from the Manhattan Project in Chicago, and just weeks away from the dropping of atomic bombs on Hiroshima and Nagasaki. The time and place of my birth have informed my entire life. When I moved to Canada, I had naively hoped for a reprieve from the interventionist policies of the US and the nuclear madness. I discovered within the first few days of my forest reverie that the US stored Genie nuclear rockets at the Canadian Forces Base Comox, a mere fifteen kilometres to my north. And sixty kilometres to the south, US nuclear-armed and powered navy vessels regularly steamed into Nanoose Bay. In the early eighties, now a Canadian citizen, I joined with others to form the Denman Island Peace Group. We resisted the testing of cruise missiles at Cold Lake; low-level military flights over First Nations lands in Sheshatshiu, Labrador, and northern BC; Star Wars; nuclear arsenal buildups; military spending; wars in Iraq, Afghanistan, the Balkans; and on and on. We met every issue with letters, art, theatre, music, research, civil disobedience and collaboration across Canada and the globe. We hired buses to take Denman Islanders to the Vancouver Peace Marches, one time having a float called The War Machine, which screamed out taped discordant sounds as it made its way over the Burrard Bridge. I was proud to be arrested with others for blocking the road into the Canadian Forces Base at Nanoose Bay with roses and loaves of bread on International Women's Day. The mischief charges were ultimately dropped, as any trial would have called attention to the base and its nuclear risks, which, in our opinion, would not have been in the government's best interests.

Also in the eighties, in a quest to understand why humans cannot seem to get along with each other and to deepen my peace activism, I enrolled in Antioch University, Ohio, to complete a distance-learning master's degree

In my dim and unheated studio, clay was my second skin. I patiently drove pots in a station wagon through a pothole maze to a neighbour's kiln. Photo Paul Bailey

in peace studies. Pre-computer, I typed my thesis on an electric typewriter perched upon my bed overlooking a pond, with quacking ducks as muses. The degree opened a door for me: I became the resource coordinator for the Pacific Campaign for Disarmament and Security. I travelled all over the

Asia-Pacific region, even to the prickly-tense demilitarized zone between North and South Korea. Our work to create a Northeast Asia nuclear-weapon-free zone remains unrealized, but we are ever hopeful. I am still a researcher for a Japanese peace organization, gathering information from the Pentagon, the White House, major US and international newspapers, US Congress and other sources to pass on to tireless peace activists in Japan. It has always been important to me to stretch beyond the shores and safety of Denman Island across oceans to create bonds with others committed to world peace, and to be a global citizen.

Another passion of mine is trees, as my neighbours will attest when I occasionally scold them for wayward chainsaw antics. When I came to Denman Island, a mere 5 percent of its exquisite landscape was protected. I joined the Denman Conservancy Association and learned about conservation covenants, land acquisition and management, fundraising and legal labyrinths. Like David, we took on Goliath when we sued a corporate clear-cutter. With allies, we have now contributed to the protection of 25 percent of Denman lands. The work continues.

In 1970 I learned that my natural habitat is a small community where people work every day to better the lives of its residents, its plants and animals, and its lands and waters. The seeds I planted early on have germinated and blossomed here. I find no discontinuity between the past, the present and the future in the trajectory my life has taken from Chicago, through Los Angeles, Berkeley and Seattle to Denman Island—metropolis to small island. I expect to stay here. One only pays to ride the ferry *to* Denman. There is a dark joke here that if one dies on the island, one doesn't have to pay the ferry fare back across Baynes Sound.

I have left the sweetest part to the last. Still living among the same trees beside the same duck pond, I have a loyal partner of twenty-eight years by my side. I have a devoted brother and sister who think I am a better person than I really am. I am blessed with a loving daughter who, like me, embraces the wonders of this earth, fashions things with her hands and cares for her daughters with tenderness. It was an entirely unanticipated blessing that she and her husband, and my two little granddaughters, now six and four, would move back to the valley, away from the neon life of Vancouver. Born in Cumberland, growing up on Denman and now living in Comox under the protection of the Beauforts, my daughter and her daughters have become the next generations of Comox Valley women.

Trusting Our Instincts

PEGGY KABUSH

Arrived in 1970

As we drove north on the Island Highway, passing through small towns in our 1965 Volkswagen van in July 1970, Denis and I wondered about our choice to live in Courtenay. We had never travelled north of Parksville but had seen an article about the Comox Valley summer music camp in a *Beautiful British Columbia* magazine. After living in Toronto and Vancouver, we were ready to leave the big cities behind and live closer to the outdoors. We had considered homesteading in northern BC, but after growing up in Vancouver, we found the draw of the ocean was strong. As a young married couple, our goals at the time were simple: starting our new jobs as teachers and finding a suitable place to live. Courtenay's downtown was small, with only two stoplights, but we were relieved to see young people in the stores, streets and parks. We were unable to find accommodation, so we decided to continue the search later in August before the school year began. Luckily, we chose to explore the waterfront roads before going back to Vancouver. We found a wonderful suite to rent in an adobe house by Kin Park, with an agreement to vacate in the summer for the owner's family.

We had planned to drive across Canada again at the end of our first year of teaching, but plans changed thanks to the Queen's visit to Courtenay at the beginning of May. Instead of waiting with the schoolchildren on Cliffe Avenue to wave to Queen Elizabeth, we decided to visit Hornby Island. The schools were closed, so we had a day off work. On Hornby we saw several lots for sale, so we returned the next weekend and found a waterfront lot for fifty-nine hundred dollars! Camping on this little island all summer was more appealing than the long drive back to Ontario. We used the three thousand dollars we had saved for our trip for the down payment and then

It was exciting for a city girl to catch three salmon from a canoe while living in a tent on Hornby Island! They were so delicious after baking in a stone pit on the beach.

paid forty dollars a month toward the remainder. The taxes were seventy-five dollars a year. We could afford it, but would not have much to live on for the summer. In the seventies, teachers didn't get paid during July and August, but we were young and carefree, so we didn't worry much about finances. We lived in a tent, cooked over an open fire, fished out of our canoe and enjoyed swimming off the rocks. Life was simple and wonderful! We spent the summer walking all the beaches, collecting lumber to build a needed stairway down to the beach. Our outhouse, which had no door and only partial walls, didn't smell and had a great view of the water. We pumped drinking water from a public well down the road. With a six-car ferry, gravel roads and a very small co-op store, there were very few tourists in 1971. Cars rarely drove down our road and also rarely would we see a swimmer at the Grassy Point beach. We went to town for groceries once a week on the ferry, which cost $2.50 for the round trip.

Completing the stairs inspired Denis to take a construction course, which then led to us building our first house outside of Comox in 1972. At that time, as a woman I did not qualify for a mortgage, but we were fortunate to borrow some money from our parents to get us started. I learned how to use the power tools and a hammer along with Denis. We made a conscious decision not to have a family because of our concerns about overpopulation and the environment. The pill and other forms of contraception gave women in the seventies a choice about motherhood. My role as a wife was changing and evolving as we worked out how to share household chores in a different way from the traditional expectations of earlier generations. This required sharing feelings and concerns, which wasn't always easy. Denis did not expect me to serve him his meals like his mother had or to do all the cleaning of the house.

In 1974 we independently started thinking about having a family but didn't tell each other for three weeks. I was twenty-eight years old but wasn't feeling the pressure of my biological clock. As I worked with and enjoyed the children at school, I realized it would be fun to have our own family. Our daughter, Danelle, was born in April 1975. Denis learned all the breathing exercises in the prenatal classes and was one of the first men to be in the operating room at the Comox Hospital.

Early in 1975, we still desired to homestead, so we searched for farmland or acreage by checking out all the ads in the *Greensheet*, the local newspaper. We could have shared a riverfront farm with friends, but we wanted to maintain our independence, so we ended up buying ten acres on Lerwick Road, which seemed quite remote at that time. Friends complained about driving up the muddy and rutted McDonald Road to visit us. We bought a mobile home so we could live on the property while we built our second house. Just before moving the mobile, Denis broke his leg in a soccer game, which meant I had to oversee the move and make arrangements for the driveway. That October it rained every day, which added to the stress, especially when I got our van stuck in the mud just before going to teach for the afternoon. Carrying Danelle, who was six months old, I had to walk a mile down the road to phone our babysitter to ask her to pick us up. As a mother, I chose to teach part-time, which meant giving up my permanent contract. However, I wasn't too concerned, since there were still many teaching positions at that time. I wanted career fulfillment and stimulation from outside the home, but not full-time work. This was the first time the school board had allowed the sharing of a teaching position. There were two other pairs of women sharing a class in 1975. In 1981 I was able to have a permanent contract as a part-time teacher.

As construction on the Lerwick house began, I had to make pipe connections and dig trenches to the new foundation while Denis took care of Danelle in the mobile home. After completing one connection to the house, I discovered that the water did not come on in our mobile, which caused us to panic. Luckily, the pebbles that had fallen into the pipe could be removed right at the junction to the mobile. Water was flowing from our well the next day. We worked as a team on sawing wood and insulating and wiring the house. I enjoyed the challenge of figuring out some of the electrical circuits. Every week we worked two evenings and on Saturday in order to move into a completed house before our son, Geoff, was born in April 1977.

Once we were living in the house, we planted a garden and fruit trees and built a chicken coop, woodshed and greenhouse. We had cleared about two acres around the house, so there were lots of trees left to cut for firewood, which we used to heat the house. We read books on self-sufficiency, ordered seeds from a catalogue and began producing almost all our food. In our large garden, we grew a variety of vegetables, raspberries, strawberries and rhubarb. August and September were busy months of making jam and canning tomatoes, pickles, peaches and pears. We eventually raised pigs and meat birds, which gave us incredible manure for the garden. We butchered the meat ourselves, which allowed us to customize the cuts to the sizes that suited our family. The hens, protected by a rooster, gave us fresh, tasty eggs every day. We bought unpasteurized milk from a farmer in Dove Creek and then made butter with the cream. We also made lard from the pork fat. All seemed so good and healthy! We joined a home-based food co-op to order large quantities of dried food and cheese. This co-op eventually became a storefront near Lake Trail School, and then later the Edible Island store.

After Geoff was born, I made very good friendships with some women who met once a week with a trained facilitator to share our past and present lives. This group originated with a Moms and Tots drop-in group at the health centre in Courtenay. It was a very important time for me to realize that my perceptions as a young woman and mother were not unique, and also that I could be different from my mother, who never shared personal feelings. Joining a women's book club in the late seventies was also significant for my social and intellectual stimulation. We met once a month to read a fiction or non-fiction book, which we discussed at the meeting. Incredibly, this group is still meeting thirty-nine years later, with the same twelve members! For physical fitness I played tennis in the summer and squash in the winter. A couple of afternoons a week, I would meet with two other mothers so we could take turns watching the kids while we played squash at the Courtenay Recreation Centre.

After taking a year off work when Geoff was born, I went back to teaching part-time to save money for Denis to go to graduate school for a master's degree in counselling. There was only one elementary school counsellor in the area at that time. When we realized we would have to move away from the Comox Valley for Denis to work as a school counsellor, we decided to instead use our savings to drive around North America and spend three months in Mexico. We camped in a small Dodge van that had a three-quarter-size bed, a small fridge and a propane stove. Danelle slept on a board that we placed over the dashboard and front seats, while Geoff slept on the floor between the seats. We built a small cupboard that held four tote trays to hold our clothes. It was a wonderful year of bonding with Danelle, who was five, and Geoff, who was three when we left in late August.

When we returned in April, we started building a small cabin on our lot on Hornby Island. We have since made two additions to the cabin, which make it a very comfortable home any time of the year. We still desire to be somewhat self-sufficient, so we have a small vegetable garden, including rhubarb from my childhood home, and several fruit trees. The ocean view remains the same, but sadly, gone are the evenings of jumping in the canoe to catch salmon, once so plentiful. They used to bubble up as they chased the herring right in our bay. We now have a house on a small lot in the Old Orchard area of Courtenay, but we spend most of our retirement days on Hornby Island, where we first purchased land and where we feel very connected to the environment and the community. We are extremely thankful that we always followed our instincts in the choices we made about where and how to live.

Deep Roots

SANDY KENNEDY
Arrived in 1970

The year is 1970 and I'm feeling so very clever. I'm living in Vancouver, a hotbed of alternative lifestyles. A couple of years prior, I'd graduated with a master's degree from the University of British Columbia and now had a great counselling job, working in an agency of smart young professionals. We positively shimmered with optimism.

Finally I was making big money, after numerous summer jobs, my worst in a Montreal potato chip factory, frenetically plucking burnt chips off a conveyor belt. I had stylish clothes, great boots and shoes, and a growing collection of leather and fringe, mandatory attire for attending weekend outdoor rock festivals. I was starting to experiment with psychedelic drugs and was having a terrific time discovering myself.

It was a long way from my prairie Ukrainian farm roots that had served me wonderfully as a child. Now I was a professional woman. Sophisticated. Chic. And mesmerized by the feminist uprising slowly permeating the culture.

So how come, only a couple of years later, gumboots now my go-to footwear, I'm covered in bramble scars and nettle stings, grubbing out a garden in the middle of a clear-cut on Denman Island?

Because in the fall of 1970, still in Vancouver, I got married, radiant in my very best hippie finery, to a most lovely red-haired Irish poet-philosopher not long removed from life in a Passionist monastery. Along with many other values I held dear, he shared my passion for nature. Many weekends we would head off in his old Volkswagen van to explore some special wilderness area. After these magical ramblings, returning to the city on Monday mornings became increasingly difficult. We hankered to spend more time in natural places, to simplify our lives, live close to the earth. We became bedazzled by the lure of self-sufficiency.

Thus began our quest for the perfect (and cheap) spot to build our lives together. After countless weekends searching for land, we came upon Denman Island (*Sla-dai-aich*). The instant we set foot on an eleven-acre property that was for sale, we knew this would be our home. It was cheap, with one corner of the acreage badly scarred, having recently been logged, but the remainder was marvellous: a vibrant forest with a valley of swordferns through which a creek flowed.

After purchasing the land, we continued working in the city for a year, saving every penny we made. On weekends we combed through junk stores and garage sales that were practically giving away beautiful old wood-framed windows, doors and bricks, old hand tools, anything old and "homesteady."

The spring of 1972 found us and our assorted junk on the tiny seven-car Denman ferry, sailing to what was to become our home and community for the next half-century.

We didn't have a clue how to use any of the hand tools. We didn't even know how to cook, but we had cleverly brought cases of canned Chuckwagon dinners and Chef Boyardee (*blush*). But that was the beauty of the whole adventure. Our practical skills were evenly matched at about zero, so we were both on a level playing field. No one was the boss. We were both strong and readily took to the heavy physical work as well as the rugged lifestyle. This was quite different from my city back-to-the-land imaginings, which had me floating about in long dresses and dreamily plucking wildflower bouquets as my partner, Des, eloquently recited nature poetry.

Clearing land for a cabin and garden was immediately in order. Smothered in thistles and brambles lay scores of felled trees remaining from a botched logging operation. Clearing the mess meant starting up the newly purchased chainsaw. Eeeek! It was a frightening beast that made a terrible racket. Even worse, in order to saw the huge cedar trunks lying felled on the ground into lumber, we needed an Alaska mill attachment, along with backs of steel. From that monstrous job, though, we amassed beautiful cedar siding, cabinetry boards, and planks for countertops, couches and beds for the "real house" we'd construct years later.

Determined to grow our own food, we prioritized burning immense piles of debris, then excavating, by hand, stumps and huge boulders to clear a patch for food production. That fifty-by-one-hundred-foot garden of virgin forest soil, rich with micronutrients and wood ash, was extremely bountiful, providing a cornucopia of healthy food. I easily took to preserving food, canning and drying jars of produce for the winter, as we had no electricity. Thanks to the benign coastal climate, root crops remained snuggled

Roughing it in the bush: Des and I exuberantly plunge into transforming a clear-cut into a whimsical homestead, one log at a time.

in the soil for fresh eating during winter. I even romantically candied borage flowers and mint leaves (I've never done it since!). We learned to supplement our diet by foraging for wild plants, enjoying enormous salads of sheep sorrel, chickweed, clover, miner's lettuce and wild violets; big plates of steamed nettles and mushrooms; bowls of thistle soup; oysters from the beach; and trout from a nearby pond.

I even cleared a little patch for a flower and herb garden, my heart yearning to have at least one tiny spot of refinement. An old photo shows me reclining in our galvanized bathing tub in that first flower garden. I am tanned and muscled, my body sprinkled in flower petals, basking in the summer sun. Gorgeous!

Evenings found us perched by a bonfire, recounting the day. We were entirely besotted with each other, with our expanding repertoire of skills and with the wondrous nature surrounding us. We basked in the freedom and expansiveness of our new lives.

Sisterhood is fanciful: the neighbourhood women and I cast off our overalls and dress up for a frolic in the hay. Photo Laura Prince

We hand-dug a twenty-foot well, and with winter bearing down, set about building a better shelter than our primitive log shack. Slated to eventually be a goat barn, the sixteen-by-twenty-four-foot structure was cobbled together using posts and beams hewed from logs, along with scavenged timbers and boards, plus thousands of hand-split cedar shakes. Suffering from chilblains in freezing temperatures, we finally finished the barn that winter solstice. The lovingly built shelter would become our home for the next seven years while we pieced together our "real house" in the valley below.

Meshing into the Denman community, with its mélange of strife and solidarity, and varied lifestyles, was a whole other challenge. With only about 250 residents, the population was small enough that one recognized every vehicle, usually a truck, that occasionally passed by, and mostly knew where it was going and why. For those who had them, telephone connections were limited to party lines. The place abounded with creative people, so all sorts of avenues opened up for expressive ventures. Soon I was studying interpretive dance, belly dancing, experimenting in theatre, singing my head off, meditating, yoga posing. I felt myself a throbbing orb of sensuality and creativity.

Wild dances in our venerable old community hall were legendary. Drinking cheap wine, smoking hand-rolled cigarettes and dope, and partying long into the night, I was giddy from being in a place of exquisite natural beauty and a community of weird and wonderful inhabitants.

I was also learning the value of collectivity. Co-ops of various kinds proliferated. Tools were shared, resources pooled, and work bees helped raise houses and harvest the hay. Volunteerism, the lifeblood of small communities, flourished, as it still does today. Learning to work together, we were creating a human environment as rich and productive as our natural setting. In our neighbourhood, we were blessed with two like-minded families with whom we shared feasts, rituals, study groups and child rearing.

Becoming politically active became hugely important for me during the seventies and continues to influence my life today. It began with concern over Denman itself. Regional government planned on zoning the whole island for small lots with a potential build-out of seventy thousand people! Thus began for me, and others of shared vision, years of meetings and protests, presenting briefs, and constant organizing to preserve Denman's rural character. Des and I and a friend started the *Denman Rag & Bone*, the island's first newspaper, which printed challenging commentary and chronicled that decade.

Our action group branched out. Soon we were tackling the Comox Valley's plan to pipe raw sewage into nearby waters, herbicide spraying on Vancouver Island, a massive log-booming facility in Baynes Sound, and the storage of nuclear warheads at Nanoose Bay and Canadian Forces Base Comox. Strong social and political ties were forged with like-minded activists in the valley and across Vancouver Island. Later on we would blockade in Strathcona Park and Clayoquot Sound, involving months of organizing, incarceration, court appearances and house arrest. A born pounding-heart scaredy-cat, I developed courage through the strong bonds of a tight group.

Though I had a loving partnership and a strong community, I also needed intimate relationships with women: close friends to share books and ideas with, a support group. Feminism was energizing my life, and I wanted to explore it with other women.

From the beginning, my reaction to island women had been intimidation. They all appeared to sew their leather outfits, knit their socks and make their pottery. They knew the difference between soy grits and buckwheat groats, and they produced delicious casseroles for the many potlucks. Meanwhile, I was going through cords of wood in the cookstove, trying to soften up dried beans (presoaking! Who knew?) and attempting to demystify macramé by kerosene lamp.

Finally I trepidatiously asked a few women if they would be interested in joining a women's group to explore feminism, and the rest is "herstory." We started with each woman taking a whole session to tell her life story. We bonded quickly, exploring new and exciting feminist territory. We learned breast self-examination and, flashlight and speculum in hand, marvelled at the beautiful differences in our vaginas and clitorises. My best potluck contribution ever was the vulva buns I individually shaped and decorated for one of our raucous annual International Women's Day festivities.

Other island women became interested, and I was asked to help start up additional groups (without the flashlight). And what nights they were, often not ending until two or three in the morning. These were child-rearing years, and roles in relationships were being challenged: a new political horizon for women was opening. They were exciting times, full of exhilaration, agony and stimulation.

A spirituality group formed; we chanted, wildly danced and fiercely howled at the moon. Even Starhawk came to visit. Denwomen's Theatre Collective was formed. We started by presenting extremely funny feminist skits, then writing and performing pieces at various women's conferences and festivals on Vancouver Island.

The Magic Bus at Port H'Kusam: I was delighted to be with joyful young feminists from Denman Island cavorting at the first-ever Women's Festival.

Offshoots of this early feminist energy on Denman and in the valley were the three legendary Women's Festivals held each summer in the mid-seventies. Seventy-five of us valley girls hiked in to Port H'Kusam for a three-day mind-blowing experience, and three years later my women's group organized for two hundred women from Vancouver Island to gloriously camp together in a hidden meadow on Denman. Rereading descriptions of some festival workshops tells of our lives back then: chainsaw maintenance, car mechanics, bannock making, salmon smoking, leg hair appreciation, sexuality, et cetera.

Near the end of the seventies, working with women created a defining life path for me. Recognizing that a structural framework was needed for women working together for change, four of us valley feminists secured a grant to establish the North Island Women's Self-Help Network. We devoted ourselves to women training and organizing for the first time in the resource-based towns from Courtenay north. Over the years, creative initiatives and women-centred organizations flourished. A huge three-volume self-help manual for empowering women in their groups and communities was produced and subsequently reprinted and distributed across Canada.

Besides all this political fervour and feminist frenzy, Des and I still had to build a proper house. Problem was, we didn't quite have the expertise for it. Our education—psychology for me, Latin and moral theology for Des—was of little use. We had no electricity, very little capital, a few basic manuals and a sorry collection of hand tools. But with no building code on the island, we could be as whimsical as we wished in our design, except there was no design. Our piles of salvaged and hand-hewn materials defined what the house would become. In the end the entire project came in at forty-five hundred dollars, with a thousand of that going to paying an electrician. We moved into our romantic little octagon mushroom of a house, with all its peaks, dormers and gables, on the winter solstice of 1978. Had we moved into a palace, we couldn't have been more pleased with ourselves. We had built the most beautiful house in the world.

Before tackling the landscaping that loomed next, we took off to roam around Europe for six months. While camping in Greece, we discovered the practical beauty of stone terracing. Back home, we took to laying local sandstone along the slope of the gentle valley in which the house sits. We used hand-split cedar posts and rails to enclose a large space around the house. Retaining old-growth cedar stumps and native species, we expanded the rock works to include pathways, steps, an alcove and a pond. Dozens of heritage roses were planted, along with numerous shrubs, grasses and ornamental trees. Almost all of the plants began as whips, seedlings or cuttings. Because they were not watered, the plants knew to put their roots down deep. Their only fertilizer comes from our compost outhouse.

Decades later, and still to our amazement, this whimsical garden and rustic home have been featured in numerous magazines, calendars and TV shows. Partly that's because Des became a published author (starting with *Harrowsmith* magazine) and TV presenter. Many of his books extolled the delights and foibles of the gardening life. As well, I started the Denman Home and Garden Tour to raise funds for our Denman Conservancy Association. There were few such tours back then, but from touring gardens in England, and knowing our island had numerous unique homes and gardens, we felt that a tour seemed like a winner. And it was: over the years, thousands of visitors have poured in, providing substantial funds for purchasing land for conservation.

The garden has filled in and matured, as have we. Like our plants, we've put down roots, as deep as nearly half a century will allow. Of an evening, we love to view the garden from its many vantage points, tea or rhubarb wine in hand—well, mainly wine—and ponder how it came to be. Luck played its part for sure. And privilege. And the help of friends and family. We still live a simple life, our values similar to when we arrived. The bulk of our food we grow and preserve. We exempt ourselves from the wiles of consumerism, buying only what we truly need. (Good grief, I'm making us sound like Ma and Pa Kettle!)

I live in a vibrant community. I am surrounded by strong women of all ages. I am still curly-toed crazy about the guy I live with, and am daily immersed in beauty. I have a powerful sense of place and am humbled that the choices I made back in the early seventies brought me to such a marvellous place to live.

I Used to Say I Was a Hippie

SUSAN HOLVENSTOT
Arrived in 1971

"We were all so optimistic back then."

~ *Frankie Rankin, host of the 1977 Women's Festival in Royston*

I was born in upper New York State, part of a white, middle-class, upwardly rising rural family. My dad, Clyde, was a mechanical engineer. My mother, Luz, was an animal rights and human rights advocate, as well as a peace activist. She raised show-quality Irish setters and ran a large boarding kennel. I remember her phoning in to weekly radio shows for the Humane Society. In 1965, when I was fifteen, I attended a huge anti-war rally in Washington, DC, with her.

After high school in New Jersey, I sort of attended the University of California, Berkeley, living in Oakland and San Francisco for two years. This was just after the 1968 People's Park takeover and the Summer of Love, in the midst of many anti-Vietnam War protests. I remember smelling tear gas and seeing the police horses as large waves of us ran through the downtown streets of San Francisco.

Two of my draft-age friends, Ken and Thom, were making their escape to Canada, settling on Vancouver Island at Oyster Bay, halfway to Campbell River. They were living in little cabins at what was then Bennett's Point Resort, now Ocean Resort Hotel and Spa. In December 1971 I came up to visit them during my winter school break. I was totally stunned by the beauty of the snow-covered mainland mountains, the ocean, the peaceful vibes and the medical plan. I didn't go back until six months later to close out my room in a co-op house.

We lived in little, wood-heated pressboard cabins on the beach. The owner hauled logs up from the beach, and he loaned us a chainsaw. A very trusting fellow! We hung out at the health food store in Campbell River, where we met Ron. He was the sole caretaker of a waterfront property with a large sawmill, Port H'kusam, near Sayward on the Johnstone Strait. He became the main organizer of the Renaissance Fair. In the spring of 1972, we moved to and fixed up abandoned buildings at Port H'Kusam, and later Rock Bay, both old steamship ports. But my social base was always the Comox Valley: for the food co-op, the music, the Arts Alliance and Renaissance Fair, and my growing circle of friends. I remember Arts Alliance dances with Pied Pumpkin, later Pied Pear: Rick on dulcimer, Shari on violin and Joe on guitar, yelling, "How come nobody's dancing?"

Others from the San Francisco Bay Area came up, and many became landed immigrants during the 1974 Amnesty Program that Canada offered. If you had lived here for at least a year, verified by as little as a postmarked letter or a library card, and hadn't broken any laws, you were in. Oh, those discussions amongst us of the US, who didn't trust the government, on whether we were willing to come forward with our real names! I had lived successfully for three years with a false social insurance number as Susan Longley of Waterloo, Ontario. I even tried to change my accent, eh? Many of us did become Canadian citizens, part of a wave of an estimated 50,000 to 125,000 immigrants motivated by opposition to the Vietnam War.

I lived at Port H'kusam for five years. I didn't know at the time that this area is considered one of the most dangerous portions of the BC coast. I learned about the tides and currents, paddling my canoe three miles north to Kelsey Bay for groceries. Sometimes I had to avoid gaping whirlpools. We ran to put canoes in the water as the cruise ships passed so we could ride the wakes. I watched the sun and moon arc over Mount H'kusam, chopped tons of firewood and rode my first horse, Kyla, over the steep mountain road to get my mail. Ron, Bernie, Katie, Thom and Jane and others lived there over the years, all in fixed-up barns, tool sheds and chicken coops.

I spent several summers camping out on Bamfield's beautiful west coast beaches with other nomads. There I met Bob, Don, Tony and Gary. They were young fishermen and would usually have a free fish to offer us. Bob, originally from California, was looking for a permanent home on the West Coast, and he eventually found Nuchatlitz, a beautiful, remote sixty-acre island near Nootka Island. I was just a beach bum and itinerant tree planter, but I was intrigued. The call to my father, a "dear daddy" call, lasted an hour. I explained that I didn't want to go to college, and would he fund part of my Nuchatlitz purchase instead? It was a lovely conversation, my dad admitting that he never had the option to do anything but college-work-marriage-kids, and he would help me. He bought into Nuchatlitz Inc. as a shareholder, and he loaned me five thousand dollars for my share in 1976.

I was wearing my Guatemalan outfit (acquired in recent travels there) at one of the many public hearings I attended. I was in Guatemala during the 1976 earthquake.

He and my mother, now separated, both came to help build the first cabin. In 1993 Olive Scott eventually became a shareholder as well.

In the summer of 1975, Don, Bernie, Arleta and I ran a business we called Skybird Fish. We fixed up an old school bus, built insulated fibreglass boxes, filled them with fresh spring salmon (the biggest ones, "smilies") and ice in Bamfield and sold them to high-end restaurants in Kamloops. Then we washed out the boxes, loaded them with organic fruit in Summerland and raced back to the coast. We sold boxes of cherries, apricots and peaches to the Arts Alliance and food co-ops. We called the fruit "unsprayed," because the term "organic" wasn't yet in use.

Although I lived in Port H'kusam, summered in Bamfield and bought into land near Nootka Island, the Comox Valley was always my social centre. I moved there in 1976, living in a little cabin on Susan Sandland's Plateau Road property. Her goat shed was the distribution centre for the Glacier Fed Food Co-op, which I volunteered with. In a year I moved to Merville, close to the first home of Edible Island. Sackville Road, opposite the Merville Store, was "upper" Merville, sandy and dry, as compared to "lower" Merville, wet and muddy, where Sally Gellard lived. I didn't really need gumboots very much. I lived in an old, wood-heated house for thirty-five dollars per month, pulled water from a well by bucket, used kerosene lamps and rode my horse to work at Edible Island.

I belonged to the Fed-Up Food Co-op network from the start in the early seventies. The co-op, with up to forty buying clubs across BC, ran a warehouse in Vancouver and bought natural foods from wholesalers. In rotation, each club sent volunteers to break down and package up the weekly orders (work week). We managed fifty-pound bags of almonds, gallons of honey, huge bags of spices, a cold warehouse and a tiny heated office in East Vancouver. Our local buying club, Ok-Why-ee Co-op, was centred out of Sunny Monday, the home of my best friends, Tim, Emma, Peter and Liz, in Black Creek. Ah, many a friendly night was spent there, sorting food, eating and making music by the wood stoves. Later came Glacier Fed Co-op. When we had too many extras, and as Fed-Up was advocating regional warehouses, we rented a large, empty space in Merville, so we could sell to the public.

When Bruce, Michael and I decided in 1979 to form Edible Island Natural Food Warehouse as a workers' co-op, my dad came through with a five-thousand-dollar loan to get us started. I taught myself bookkeeping, and we ran it for two years before paying anyone. Later came Sally Gellard, Mary Ann, Ruthie, Sylvia, Sue and Gary and many more. We sold to the

Renaissance Fair booths and even had our own truck for North Island deliveries. Later, Edible moved to downtown Courtenay, first on upper Fourth Street, then opposite the Sid Williams Theatre, sharing space with the first vegetarian restaurant in town, the Bar None Café, and now in the old BC Hydro building. I am proud to have been a founder of one of the best and longest-lasting businesses in the Comox Valley.

One may wonder how we ran Edible without paying anyone. Many of us planted trees seasonally and could then collect unemployment insurance over the winter. I worked for the Canadian Forest Service in Squamish for $4.50 per hour. I worked with Skookum Co-operative for fifteen to thirty cents per tree, with Cara Tilston, Devaki Johnson, Gwyn Sproule, Josephine Peyton, Joanie, Sean, Liz and many more. I loved camping out and got to see a lot of incredible scenery around the province. At the top of a run, I could step into the ancient forest that edged all our cutblocks, and imagine what the intact forest looked like. I liked the work, even with its rain, blackflies and smelly "dry tent." The food and companionship was good, and where else could I earn up to a hundred dollars per day?

Some of us have been trying to remember the dates and locations of the Comox Valley Women's Festivals. Here is what I make of it. I hosted the first one in 1976 at Port H'kusam, close to Sayward. We had to walk in over a three-mile-long road. About forty women came. The next was at Comfort Soap Farm in Royston, hosted by Frankie. In 1981 it was at Forbidden Plateau Lodge when Gwyn was living there. Later, on Denman Island and in Errington, I attended at least two of them. I remember the satisfaction of teaching women to use a chainsaw, a skill I had only recently mastered. We had guest presenters. Elder and herbal master Norma was one. Bonfires, music, nudity, fun and learning: a Women's Festival!

In 1982 I bought into my shared land in Dove Creek, north of Courtenay, and hand-built a pole house. Later a cob-and-straw-bale house was built on my portion of the land. I've happily lived, worked, gardened, hiked and kept my hand in social and political activism here for the last thirty-five years. I consider it my good luck to have found and enjoyed the beautiful Comox Valley and Vancouver Island for all these years.

I used to say I *was* a hippie. Shucks, in 1969 I even went to Woodstock, as I was living close by in New Jersey. Now I more often say I *am* a hippie, still striving for that low-key, peaceful, sustainable and politically engaged life.

Merville Musings

GERRI MINAKER
Arrived in 1971

Spring 1971. My husband, Barry, and I were living in student housing at the University of British Columbia. I was working in the library, he was finishing up the school year and we were chomping at the bit to be free. We had dreams and visions. For a few years, we had known people who had moved from Vancouver to rural locations. It was the seventies, and lots of our contemporaries were eager to explore a new way of living: on the land, close to nature, free from the consumerism that seemed to dominate our urban culture. We wanted to "drop out."

Finally school was over. We packed up our 1951 Pontiac with all our worldly goods, plus our two cats, Pippin and Sam, and ventured east from Vancouver to the Kootenays, where we had friends who were living "on the land." For the next few weeks, we scoured the Kootenays, up country roads, down pathways through the woods, looking for deserted cabins, homesteads, chicken shacks: anything that could be made habitable. Our main priorities were that it had to be rural and suitable for gardening. It was all to no avail. Every hollow stump had several hippies living in it.

We ran out of cash and returned to Vancouver to access some savings we had in the bank, and then we headed out again. This time our destination was the Cariboo, where we also had friends, hoping we would have better luck there. On the way out of Vancouver, my husband took a hasty left turn at a stoplight, causing a motor vehicle accident. The woman whose car we hit agreed to an on-the-spot settlement for the damage. We paid her out of our rapidly depleting cash, and to make ourselves feel better, we decided to take a ferry boat ride to Vancouver Island instead of a long road trip to the Cariboo. Up to that point, Vancouver Island hadn't even occurred to us as a place to settle.

We camped that evening on the beach just north of Nanaimo. The next day, we headed up Island, with no particular destination in mind, again checking out side roads and any other sites that looked promising as likely places to live. North of Courtenay, at Merville, we were pulled over by the RCMP for travelling too slowly, no doubt because of all the side roads we were checking out. He gave us a warning and let us go. Having been pulled over at Merville, we decided that fate had decreed we would travel down the next side road. At the very end of the road, we parked the car.

Across a hand-built swinging bridge over the Tsolum River, we came upon paradise. In front of us was a very large acreage, with fields and paths winding between six or seven vacant cabins that were scattered about. All were empty and no one seemed to be in charge. I remember it was a lovely mid-May evening; the birds were chirping, the sun was just setting: I felt like the seeking had ended.

We camped that night and the next day made inquiries at the nearest neighbours about who owned the property and what the story was. We were told that it had recently been sold to someone in Victoria. Up until that time, the property had belonged collectively to a group of Catholic men, mostly priests, who had bought it in the mid-sixties in order to establish a hermitage. They had built individual, modest cabins and were living a meditative, simple life. After a time, the collective had dissolved and the participants had moved on. We drove down to Victoria to discuss renting, and the owner agreed that we could rent whichever cabin we desired for twenty-five dollars a month. We returned to Merville, chose a cabin and moved in.

Within a few months, all the cabins were occupied by fellow roving hippies. Some were draft dodgers, escaping the insanity of America's involvement in the Vietnam War, and some were urban friends of ours who came to visit and stayed. Suddenly, we had an instant commune.

That summer I was living the dream. We cultivated a garden and grew vegetables for the first time. Being a city girl, I had no idea what a turnip looked like in the ground, how parsley grew, when a pea was ripe for picking. Everything was a learning experience and an adventure. Hauling water from the river for drinking, and learning to can fruit: all was magical. I recall my first attempt at canning. Someone had brought several cases of fruit from the Okanagan, and Beth and I decided to preserve it all for winter. We managed to gather a canning pot, jars and lids, but had no idea how to proceed from there. By trial and error, hours and hours later, we had canned the entire lot. Three times a week I would walk a half-hour to a farm where I could buy fresh milk. I also learned to identify wild mushrooms, chop firewood and pick salal, used by florists in floral arrangements, for cash. Summer afternoons were spent swimming nude in the bucolic Tsolum River and lazing on its banks. These were big adventures for an urban girl like me.

One of the hermits from the original Hermitage still lived just off the property in his hand-built cabin. He would come over occasionally and talk to us about a simple, contemplative life. He was middle-aged (ancient in our eyes), from France, and had lived and worked as a priest in various places in France and Africa. He had eventually found himself here, in Merville, establishing the Hermitage with like-minded fellow Catholics, and his ideals were very close to ours: to get closer to nature, and to be as self-sufficient as possible. He inspired us.

That Thanksgiving, we hosted a huge dinner party at the Hermitage. We invited friends from Vancouver, new folks we'd met in the Comox Valley and just about anyone else we could think of. We killed many chickens from our flock (another new skill) and folks brought salmon, duck and bounty from their gardens. We ate like royalty and danced and sang throughout the weekend.

Winter came. It was a cold winter for the Comox Valley, and we struggled to bring in enough firewood to keep us warm. In January our first daughter was born. The hospital was twenty kilometres away and we had no working vehicle. However, our neighbours on "the other side" of the swinging bridge did. So, at 2 a.m., we traversed the snowy, slippery, swinging bridge to our neighbour's house, drove to the hospital in an old, beat-up car, along icy roads, and all went well. In those days, we just assumed everything would work out.

In the spring our collective ventured into husbandry. We bought, for cheap, a goat named Jenny, who had only one teat, in order to provide milk and cheese. None of us had ever milked a goat before, let alone a goat with a single teat, but we persevered and were soon providing ourselves with milk and delicious cheese.

We lived at the Hermitage for nearly two years, and then moved into our own handmade tipi just a bit downriver. We had hand-sewn and painstakingly hand-painted it on the outside, and we loved it. In the early spring, just after we moved in, there was a torrential rainstorm. The combination of the rainstorm and the snowmelt on the mountains caused the Tsolum River to rise. We rolled up the bottom of our tipi, filled some wheelbarrows

Home sweet home—our hand-painted tipi on the banks of the Tsolum River.

with our belongings and, with the help of friends, wheeled out to higher ground. A few days later we were able to return. We built a makeshift sauna on the banks of the river and lived there happily in our tipi the rest of the spring and summer.

Come fall, though, we decided to move back to Vancouver for employment and study opportunities. For the next two years, we couldn't get the rural lifestyle and the beauty of living close to nature out of our souls.

In 1975 we moved back to the Island, to Bowser, about forty miles south of Merville, and in 1977 we bought property just up the road from where we had first landed at the Hermitage. We hauled out our old tipi, set it up on our newly acquired land and proceeded to build a home. Here again, we were in new territory, largely unschooled in house building but, with the help of many books, some knowledgeable friends and a can-do attitude, mixed with a healthy dose of naïveté, our house gradually emerged. I was nine months pregnant and lifting heavy cedar beams in place for floor joists when my waters broke and, that evening, we welcomed our third daughter into the world. Two years after starting our house, we finally moved in. It was unfinished inside and out, but it was habitable and it was ours. We have been here for thirty-seven years. Eventually, we got the house finished, land cleared, gardens cultivated, chicken houses and horse stables built and sheep pastures created.

Wonderful, lifelong friendships have resulted. Moving to a smaller community, "back to the land," was, for me, the right decision. I have learned so much. How fulfilling it is to live close to nature and embrace a relatively simple lifestyle. My community has sustained me through good times and bad. I am part of a women's group that has been together for twenty-five years. We meet every other week and listen to and support each other. My friends and neighbours live in unique houses, hand-built by folks, like us, who knew very little about rural life in the beginning. I love to visit these homes: each is an expression of the individuals who envisioned and then created them. Gardens, too, are all one of a kind, with incredible floral beds and landscaping and abundant vegetable plots.

My four daughters, all grown now, thrived here. They still retain relationships with people, both young and old, that they knew growing up. In the early years, there were great community dances. Families turned up, everyone danced, kids were put to sleep under tables and in corners amid stacks of coats, and we frolicked into the night. There was always a loving person to entrust the children to as needed, for a few hours or even for a few nights. It was a supportive environment for parenting.

I still spend time on the Tsolum River. To me, it represents the heart of Merville. I swim in it, sometimes with my grandchildren, and walk its beautiful banks. I am grateful that fate led me to this wonderful place I call home.

The Island, 1971

SALLY GELLARD
Arrived in 1971

The ferry docks in Nanaimo in June 1971. A light rain welcomes us to Vancouver Island, and I manoeuvre Blu, our trusty VW van, north along the Island Highway. On board with me are a husband and two dogs. We're heading for a creek that flows into the Strait of Georgia on the east shore of Vancouver Island. He's been given a tank and equipment to study salmon smolts at a fisheries research station; his thesis is that mercury kills salmon.

We're equipped and ready. He has an axe, a machete, a saw, knives, buckets, rain gear, canvas tarps, sleeping bags, a compass, matches and a copy of the *Wilderness Survival Handbook*. I have new gumboots, lentils, brown rice and Virginia Woolf's *A Room of One's Own* tucked into my bag.

Rolled, wrapped and strapped up on the roof rack is The Tipi. It is the result of weeks of preparation, constructed in our North Vancouver apartment; it was sewn on my trusty Singer treadle machine, leaving shards of broken needles in its wake. The huge sewn canvas had been measured and cut into a circle at the local school gym. We carefully followed the detailed instructions for "How to Make a Tipi" in the *Mother Earth News* 1, no. 1 (January 1970), with its encouraging description: "The Plains Indian tipi is absolutely the finest of all movable shelters."

Tipi life appeals to my sense of nomad. My early life was spent moving between countries and cities, our family following my explorer/adventurer father, whose philosophy was that "home is where you hang your hat." For me, this childhood was sometimes exciting and sometimes sad. I said good-byes too often to special places and best friends.

Karen and I were ten years old, best friends forever, both leaving Trinidad at the same time: Karen to the US and me to Canada. We made a vow to join up in Niagara Falls. A picture on our school wall in Trinidad professed it

Sarah and me with my sister, Susan, on the land in Merville, 1979.

to be the place where the two countries joined. Three years later, when I finally convinced my parents to go to Niagara Falls, I searched for her among the crowd. I couldn't believe she wasn't there.

During lonely times, books had been my passion. As a teen, I turned to stories of real-life adventurers, *The Kon-Tiki Expedition*, *Robinson Crusoe* and the stories of Amelia Earhart and Albert Schweitzer, mixed in with poetry for the spirited heart. I was primed with a romantic sense of adventure.

We head north on the Island Highway, and I have no idea what lies ahead, but the open road excites me and June is a gentle time on Vancouver Island. We pull in, drive down a dirt track at Rosewall Creek and get out to explore. The logging road weaves past huge old maples laden with hanging veils of moss. We find a gravel bar beside the creek, where the flow slows, forming a pool of turquoise green. The ground here looks flat enough, dry enough and large enough to fit our camp, and over the next day, we set about levelling an eighteen-foot-diameter area to set up the tipi.

Rosewall Creek, now a provincial park just south of Fanny Bay, was then the closest thing I'd ever seen to wilderness. I am in awe of the silence under the huge trees. I stand on the bank of this creek, cedar branches swishing in the current, and taste the sweet, pure water. I didn't know water could taste like that; it was nothing like what came out of the tap in Don Mills, Ontario. As I wash my face in the ice-cold flowing water on that first day, I imagine I am the first human to set foot on what feels like an empty land. I have no knowledge, no awareness of the First People, whose land this is, who have lived here and gathered here for thousands of years before the arrival of my ancestors, which changed everything. I am conscious only of a personal sense of my discovery of this beauty.

Over the next days, we search for trees, lodgepole pine preferred, according to the *Mother Earth News* instructions. I learn West Coast tree identification skills: red cedar, spruce, fir, hemlock and pine. We cruise up and down countless logging roads and walk into the bush of second-growth forest, encountering relics of rusted trucks, deer skeletons and piles of tin cans and brown beer bottles, reminders of the last wave of loggers who had taken out the grand old-growth forests of this corner of the Island. We choose and fell our needed poles and carry them back to our site, and then I learn the art of peeling seventeen poles, each twenty-five feet long.

For five months we call this place home, and we are sustained on oysters and clams from Mud Bay and cheeseburgers from the Fanny Bay Inn.

I leave every second week, hitchhiking back and forth to my job as a counsellor with street kids in Vancouver. The contrast between my worlds is stark and exhilarating.

I fall in love with the Island, her trees and rivers, her healing and generosity. I make a promise to myself to return and so I do, along a crooked path that takes me away from city life to the outermost western edge of Vancouver Island.

Eight years later I arrive back in the Comox Valley. This time I come as a single mom, with my two-year-old daughter. I am seeking a home, cheap land and community. Good fortune brings us a family of like-minded people, and in 1979 we find and share a small parcel of forest, bush and swamp in Lower Merville.

Since then, Merville has become my permanent hat rack, and we have created a home and community close to another sweet Island river, the Tsolum. The Island continues to nurture my restless, hungry roots.

Finding Home

CARA TILSTON
Arrived in 1971

It all started with a Greyhound bus ride with my sister, up the West Coast from California to Vancouver in the summer of 1971. Having finished high school several years previously in the north of England, close to Liverpool, I had taken a nanny job in Los Angeles for a year. The trip with my sister took place a year later to celebrate her graduation from high school. A few weeks earlier, on a cheap flight over from London, we had met some people from Vancouver who told us amazing stories about the area, specifically Vancouver Island. We were keen to visit.

On my first day in Vancouver, while visiting the people we had met on the plane, I met a Canadian man who was to become the father of my first daughter. He had friends in the Comox Valley and suggested that we ride our bikes there. In 1971 the Old Island Highway was pretty quiet, and it didn't take us very long to arrive at the end of a gravel road in Merville. We were greeted by a family of American draft dodgers living in a rustic cabin, sharing the lifestyle I had hoped to find. There, on this large acreage, people were living in school buses, cabins and tipis, with no electricity or running water, sharing gardens and cooking on wood-burning or propane stoves.

We spontaneously decided to stay and not go back to the city, and our friends took us to a co-operative piece of land called the Hermitage, where we rented a tiny round house on the Tsolum River for twenty dollars a month. Seventh-day Adventists had been living on the land, and now there were several families renting from them, mostly living in cabins and tipis.

In 1973 I found out I was pregnant with my eldest daughter, Jacy. Her father and I had amicably separated, so I briefly went back to England and Wales, only to return when I was nine months pregnant. I moved back to the Hermitage to live in what was once the old church. This dwelling was separated from the rest of the 160 acres by a swing bridge that crossed the

Me with a very young Thea, probably at the Renaissance Fair.

river. I joined a great community of people with similar values and beliefs. We shared gardens, vehicles, animals and the raising of our kids.

I was a happy single parent, living the lifestyle I had always dreamed of. One evening, when Jacy was four months old, we were having a potluck dinner with my sister, who was visiting from Amsterdam. The old, airtight wood stove was burning hot. Someone went outside and started shouting. We ignored him until he came running back inside the church, screaming "Fire!" I was not used to burning wood, and apparently the green wood had built up so much creosote that it had created a chimney fire. Rushing outside, we could see that the flames were leaping all over the old shake roof. Mobilizing, we ran to the river with buckets, and someone climbed onto the roof with a chainsaw to try to cut away the burning areas. Others ran up the road to the nearest telephone, which was a good few hundred yards away. At this point, I ran back into the church, threw Jacy's crib and some of her clothes outside and tucked her away underneath my shirt. We all then went and sat on the swing bridge and watched this magical place burn down to the ground. The fire engine arrived just in time to save the outhouse.

I could only carry around twenty trees at a time at this tree-planting job. Each tree was so heavy and bulky, with roots at least a foot long!

A friendly touch on my back aroused me to the present, as I was in another state of mind, watching the propane tank explode from the heat of the fire. She asked where the baby was, and as I unwrapped my shawl to show her a breastfeeding Jacy, she offered us her home, the first cabin on the other side of the river, for us to take comfort. When I had gone back into the burning church earlier to collect Jacy, I had looked around, knowing that I was going to lose everything else left inside, and I had quickly picked up a bag of pot. Now was the time to share and tell stories about the evening's goings-on. Of course, the news of the fire spread fast, and soon there was a crowd of people gathered to hear the story, happy to see us alive and well.

This woman and her family and friends had recently bought the Hermitage and were starting to move in. What an interesting time to get acquainted! She and her family offered us food, clothes and a bed. I can honestly say that I truly loved her from the moment that she offered me motherly love while sitting on the swing bridge, watching the church, my home, burn down to the ground, until the day she died two years ago at the age of ninety.

For the rest of the summer of 1974, Jacy and I lived in a tipi on the banks of the Tsolum River, and in the fall we flew back to England for my parents' twenty-fifth wedding anniversary. We ended up staying there for two years, living on the top of a mountain in North Wales. The pull to come back home to Merville became so insistent that upon arriving back here in 1976, I knew that this was my spiritual and practical home. I was here to stay.

By 1978 tree planting had become a way of life, consistent with my values, beliefs and lifestyle. While working at a remote camp, I met the father of my younger daughter, Thea,

Me and Baby Jacy, walking past the church that burned down in the spring of 1974.

who was born in 1979. We had a beautiful home birth attended by a nineteen-year-old friend who was a lay midwife and also the daughter of the woman who had taken us in after the fire. Serendipitous!

While our children were young, they were raised in camps during the tree-planting season. We shared child care with other families, as well as cooking, planting and communal living. After every spring season, we set up another camp, this time at the Courtenay Fairgrounds, where we staffed the kitchen for the annual Renaissance Fair. This became a traditional event until 1984, when the last fair took place.

Fast-forward to 2010: I bought two acres of land with a house on the Tsolum River in Merville at the old Headquarters townsite. Jacy, her son Aiden and I walked the land, and I could point out exactly where we had lived in the tipi on the river in 1974, before houses, and acknowledge that we had come full circle. The powerful energetic pull of this land still draws my family in, and I have now lived here for eight years with the knowledge that my children and grandchildren will continue to care for this land as much as I do.

To this day, the images of flames are real and powerful, the love sustained between friends from that era to the present remains strong and our community continues to thrive. I cannot imagine living anywhere else that offers me the connections, love and sense of belonging that I have here in Merville.

Early Childhood Education in the Comox Valley

LEE BJARNASON
Arrived in 1972

I often wonder what road my life would have taken if I had not found the Comox Valley. My family had moved to Campbell River from Prince Rupert while I was in college, and I wanted to spend some time with them before considering job offers. The few trips I made to Campbell River had convinced me that Vancouver Island was magical.

While enjoying the northern Vancouver Island summer in 1972, I noticed an ad in the local paper seeking a qualified early childhood educator for a daycare centre in Courtenay. I thought, *What do I have to lose? Might as well apply.* At that time in British Columbia, there were not many qualified educators in the field of early childhood, particularly in smaller communities, so I figured I might have a chance. My interview was on a bright and sunny August day; as my mother and I drove down Mission Hill, Cat Stevens' song "Morning Has Broken" came on the radio, setting a musical backdrop to the view before us, and convincing me this was a sign.

The interview went well. I had a strong vision of what quality daycare should look like, and I wanted to put this into action. The Comox Valley Children's Day Care Society, a non-profit run by a board, was going into its second year of operation with one centre, the Merry Andrew Day Care, operating out of the bottom of St. George's United Church. It was the only daycare in the valley, and both daycare and preschool were offered. To make this even more interesting, a small group of deaf preschool children were going to have a class just off the main daycare room with their teacher of the deaf, Jean, and would spend some of the time with their typical peers. I didn't realize until many years later that we were practising inclusion before research established the benefit of having children with diverse needs playing and learning together.

I was inspired when I moved to a community where creativity, music and the arts defined the environment and were encouraged by those around me.

Many of the daycare staff were experienced with children, but I was the only qualified ECE. It was fortunate that there was some trust in me, although with some skepticism at times, as the staff were all older than me, at age twenty-one. I had strong ideas of what good daycare should look like and I thought everyone should feel the same way.

When I moved to the valley, I knew no one. Not one friend. No ideas of where to look for like-minded people. The early childhood care community was great, and while I was happy enough, I was a bit lonely and I continued to go to Vancouver for fun. However, during the following years, the Comox Valley Arts Alliance began taking form. The challenge of my work and the beauty of the valley brought me here, but it was the friends and the Arts Alliance that made me want to stay and that created a community for me.

Many wonderful people entered my life, through both the Arts Alliance and the daycare centre. We were recruiting new staff, and a woman who had recently emigrated from California with her family applied for a job at the centre. Bobby had a great background in working with children and she was hired. We soon became good friends as well as colleagues. I felt compelled to teach her how to pronounce words like a Canadian and to

My mother was always an inspiration, and she encouraged me to venture out and move to a community where I knew no one and could define myself for who I was.

accompany her on her inaugural drive in the snow. Although I didn't know how to drive, I was experienced in being a passenger on icy rides! Despite my arrogance, we remain close friends.

One day a man named Nick came to the daycare, introduced himself and asked if he could borrow some scissors to use for a children's art class he was teaching on Saturdays at the Arts Alliance. He had recently moved to the Comox Valley from the States and had such a strong Pittsburgh accent, I had a difficult time understanding half of what he said. Little did I imagine that I was going to end up living with him for most of my life. I still do!

Over the next few years, several more early childhood centres began operating in the valley. Many of the centres were developed by the Comox Valley Children's Day Care Society, with help from June, a woman from England with a strong vision for the need for licensed, quality child care. Merry Andrew Day Care (now called Lighthouse Early Learning), Rainbow Nursery School (later taken on by the Courtenay Recreation Centre and renamed Cozy Corner) and Comox Day Care (now known as Tigger Too) were some of these centres. J. Puddleduck Daycare, the first and only parent co-operative in the valley, began operation under the direction of Linda. North Island College recognized the need for licensed qualified early childhood educators and began offering evening courses in early childhood education in the early seventies, increasing the number of qualified personnel. There were certainly many other early childhood centres offering great child care, but I cannot remember them all.

In 1978 I was offered a position at the Comox Valley Child Development Centre as a support worker. The centre, then called the Comox Valley Cerebral Palsy and Neurological Association, was located in Cumberland and had begun operation in 1974. June was also instrumental in the development of this valuable resource and was a founding member. I was excited to work there, as I had a strong interest in working with children with disabilities.

My first introduction to Cumberland was by chance in the early seventies; while out for a drive with friends on a logging road, we arrived in the village. None of us had been there before. We felt like we were in a time warp and were fascinated by the architecture and beautiful surroundings. I loved it immediately and later, when walking up Camp Road to go to a batik workshop at Judith's house, I knew I wanted to live on Camp Road. Camp Road is at the end of Dunsmuir Avenue, the main street of Cumberland. My wish was finally granted in 1978 when my friend Anne asked Nick and me to rent her house on Camp. We eventually bought it and ended up living there for thirty-seven years and raising our children there; both our grandchildren were born on Camp Road.

I have now lived in all three of the main communities in the Comox Valley (Courtenay, Comox and Cumberland) and have friends from Oyster River to Mud Bay. I never tire of the beauty and the wonderful, talented and interesting friends and acquaintances I have met. I began my career in early childhood education here and will soon retire from my position as an infant development consultant at the Comox Valley Child Development Association. I still feel passionate about my work! Although I was born in Vancouver and lived in Prince Rupert, I realize that I truly grew up in the Comox Valley. The community, friends, work, culture and politics shaped me and developed the person I am and the values I have today. I have been fortunate.

I Kept Coming Back

DEVAKI JOHNSON
Arrived in 1973

Heathrow Airport, 1969: in stiletto heels, miniskirt and bouffant hairdo, with two hundred dollars in my pocket, I boarded a plane to Toronto, with no idea what was ahead. I naively bumped around Toronto in all the wrong places and somehow found myself in a lovely rooming house on Ward's Island, with the Toronto skyline's shimmering reflection on the lake between us. If I missed the morning passenger ferry, a friend would canoe me to downtown Toronto, where I worked, illegally, and ironically, for lawyers on Bloor Street. Not a landed immigrant at the time, I worked through an agency. In the evenings I volunteered at the crisis centre in Rochdale College, an extremely alternative college.

On April Fool's Day 1973, I spontaneously, with friends, left Toronto, headed on the highway for the West Coast, of which I had heard lots. Canada was still in the grips of winter, and we dug ourselves out of snowbanks more than once. Windy Winnipeg: I had never experienced cold like that before, nor have I since. It was a silly time to cross Canada, but we made it.

Once on Vancouver Island, the city girl was transformed: gumboots, jeans, wool, no bouffant under the toque. When we arrived in the Comox Valley, I was absolutely overwhelmed by all the trees—so many trees, with not much else other than flashes of houses here and there. It was too much, at the time, for us city folks, so we went back to the mainland. Vancouver in the seventies was opening up to the New Age cultural awakenings. The World Symposium with Bernard Jensen, Stephen Gaskin and Rolling Thunder was held at the Hyatt Regency, for three days on three floors, with breastfeeding in the hallways, healing sessions in many rooms and quite the aroma! I do believe the Hyatt Regency was not prepared at all for the spectacle in what was, at the time, a first-class hotel.

I was living in an older Kitsilano home with a few others, and we all had waterbeds; it's a wonder the house didn't fall over. There was lots of music, folk festivals, rock concerts. There I met Arthur, who became very significant in my life.

I returned to the Comox Valley when I was invited to a wedding at Point Holmes; there were a lot of people there. During the three days of celebration, we spent some time in Courtenay. Back then, you could slowly drive down Fifth Street and stop in the road to talk to someone in a car going the other way; there was no traffic, and it was all small and very quiet, with very friendly townsfolk. After a week we went back to Vancouver.

While I was taking an astrology course, my teacher read my chart and told me to be very careful and to not take risks for six weeks. Despite her warning, Arthur and I went on a camping trip up in the mountains between Squamish and Pemberton, with our two dogs. We got caught in a rock slide, which sent us, in the truck, hurtling two hundred feet down the mountainside. We both survived, me with a broken femur, Arthur with a scratch on his head. Both dogs were unfortunately, or fortunately, killed instantly.

We landed in the river, with water running through the cab. It took seven hours to rescue me, and even as I experienced a new threshold of pain, I realized how extremely lucky we were. I was taken first to Squamish Hospital and then transferred to Vancouver General, where I lay with my leg in traction for the next three months. My astrology teacher would visit, bringing me books to carry on my studies; it was a good opportunity, and I lived to die another day.

After I recovered from the accident, Arthur and I moved to the Comox Valley. We rented a house on Muir Road and settled into valley life. I worked in Jo's health food store in a funky old building on Cliffe and Sixth, which has since been torn down. I think that it was, at the time, the only health food store in the valley. Jo, then in her seventies, was an original pioneer in the Comox Valley; she and her friends formed a co-op years before any others. I learned a lot about health, diet and nutrition from Jo. The store was very tiny, yet it had everything; it was packed floor to ceiling and had the most amazing aroma of herbs and health.

Spending weekends hiking and camping in the mountains and hiking the endless trails around the valley, I got way more comfortable with all the trees, so many trees.

The Arts Alliance was formed and housed on McPhee Avenue. Island artists displayed their art, read poetry, made music and organized dances and movie nights; there was always something going on. The Good Day Café was started at the Arts Alliance, and I would often volunteer in the kitchen. That was where my core group of friends, including my very special friend Cara Tilston, was formed. We are all good friends to this day.

Alas, in 1976 Arthur and I broke up. At the same time I was offered a job at the Fort Health Manor by a local doctor who practised hypnotherapy for obesity and other health issues. The Fort has a long history in Comox Valley; it sits on McCutcheon's Point in Comox. From there, you can see up and down the strait and look across at the Beaufort Range. First Nations people once fortified the point against attacks from all sides, and a lot of gatherings were held there. An English gentleman had a manor built there in 1938, surrounded by thirteen acres of forested land, and he named his estate the Fort. That manor eventually became a luxury hotel, and then a private hospital for the elderly before the doctor purchased it for his practice.

I was so excited to move into a small log cabin in the forest, keeping the doctor's clients occupied while they were fasting, and teaching them about plant-based diets when they were not. The manor was amazing, with exotic wooden floors, a staircase and a lot of windows. The decor reeked of Victorian England. Sometimes, when alone there, I would roam the big house and just absorb the feeling: the attics were filled with the ghosts of the past, just a little creepy.

Eventually the good doctor had to move his business to California, where the populace was more receptive of new and alternative ways of healing. The Fort's manor still stands today, now surrounded by modern new homes instead of forests. It was a privilege to live there; I was blessed.

I then moved to Bridges Road, on the outskirts of Courtenay, and three friends and I rented a lovely big old farmhouse, which was originally a dog kennel called the Doggy Hotel, with a big sign on the highway. The owners lived in Vancouver and were very tolerant of our gatherings, healing circles, stick dancing and yoga, an alternative movement in full swing.

I met a fellow called Blue Jay at the Arts Alliance (I never did learn his real name). He had a passion for writing, and he created a small newspaper called the *New Age Dawn*; the paper had mostly New Age articles, interviews and artists. I volunteered to set all the type at a local printer, and my pal Valerie and I would, every month, drive in our beat-up Valiant to Santa Cruz in California to deliver the paper and partake in yoga/healing sessions.

I had met some tree planters and knew immediately that was what I wanted to do. There were not many crews operating at that time, and I called them all. They were mostly all-male crews, and as a woman it was hard to get accepted for such a strenuous job. I had almost given up when I got a call from Dan to plant and/or cook for Nahanni Reforestation, starting in a month. Finally!

I felt like I had won the jackpot when, at the same time, I got into a squatters' cabin down a four-kilometre trail through the forest from the Merville Store; it had a wood stove and an outhouse, was off the grid and there was zero rent—oh, happy day. I was living the dream in gumboots. There were a few of these old squatters' cabins on Crown land around the valley at that time.

Living the dream in gumboots. Photo Arthur Brockman

However, at first I was so scared of the dark, of the bogeyman, I would go to bed before dark. Eventually I had no option but to face the trail in the dark, my heart thumping all the way: nothing happened, and I lived to die another day. After that the bogeyman disappeared. I shared the cabin with Kathy and Richard, so it would be lived in while I was away travelling. We couldn't leave it too long, or someone else would take it over.

The train from Vancouver to Prince George was full of tree planters, and experienced guys teased the greenhorns like myself with horror stories, which I later found out were actually true. What a harsh reality tree planting was: the most adventurous, challenging and physical job I ever had, not at all the romantic job I had envisaged. I loved and hated it; it was heaven and hell. I never thought I could plant a thousand trees in a day, which was necessary to keep the job. But I did.

Rumbling around the logging roads in crummies was breathtaking, but it was also horrific to see the devastation of forests, logged blocks one after another; it was heartbreaking. Camp cook was a hard job too; I was first up and last to bed, isolated, usually dealing with a bear or two as well as kids and dogs. I had to haul water from creeks and keep a wood stove going for hot water. Despite it being such a tough job, at the end of the season I felt so good, physically fit and proud of having planted all those trees, a replenished forest. Despite the harsh environment and hard work, most of

Happy hippie daze! Photo Arthur Brockman

us were always keen to start again the next year. When planting season was over, I would head back to the valley to recuperate in the cabin.

Vancouver had top musical bands, many gatherings and, for me, astrology; hence, I took many ferry rides. With the Arts Alliance and the Renaissance Fair becoming more popular, more cultural events started happening in the valley. At first, local politicians were very negative about the Renaissance Fair, until Ann went to local businesses to get their opinion on whether the influx of people helped or hindered their business. The business people overwhelmingly agreed the fair was excellent, and the political attitude changed. We were so lucky to have the Renaissance Fair, organized by many of my friends, in the valley. I worked in several booths, volunteering here and there, and read astrology in Bunky's booth. The fair was so special; it brought together the whole community and Islanders from all walks of life.

I have always had a white German shepherd; I still do. Just prior to the tree-planting season, Valerie and I drove one last time to Santa Cruz to deliver the *New Age Dawn*. We stopped in Vancouver at the Naam for supper; my Katy Dog was outside, and in a flash, she was gone! We spent two days looking for her, with no luck, and then reluctantly headed south.

After tree planting some six months later, we were at the Naam again, when the waitress recognized me and gave me the telephone number of the man who had Katy Dog. He lived on Read Island, off Quadra Island, and he agreed that I could go visit.

Planters headed to the cookshack after work, but I always headed straight to the hot tub. The water was only changed once a day, so the first one in got the cleanest bath. Photo Signy Cohen

I hitched to the Heriot Bay Inn on Quadra and soon found a willing person to boat me over to Read Island to visit with Katy Dog. She was living a very happy life with her new family and a litter of pups, and so I left her there, with permission from her new owners to go visit any time. Some months later I got a call from Read Island to say I could have Katy back, if I wanted, and of course I did! Once reunited, we were together until she died at age fourteen. She loved tree-planting adventures right to the end.

Revolutionary changes were everywhere in those days: the women's movement with issues about equality coming to a head, the anti-Vietnam-War movement, logging protests. Times were changing; people were speaking out. In the seventies, in that era long before cellphones, word of mouth announced parties, gatherings, great dances at the Merville and Dove Creek halls, Women's Festivals, and many potlucks and work parties.

Life was fast paced: I was tree planting all over BC, island-hopping, teaching and learning astrology. I hitchhiked everywhere, both on and off the Island. Cabin life in between junkets was teaching me to like isolation and the challenge of being alone and comfortable with it.

I spent time with a boyfriend on Maurelle Island, who lived in a very isolated place in a pyramid that he had built, off grid with a trickling creek creating some power for lights at night. The off-grid island folks were tough, determined and motivated people, dependent on boats, tides and moons, float planes and barges bringing supplies in, no local store. They also depended on each other. My four-kilometre walk to the cabin didn't seem so bad after living on Maurelle.

I gave up the lovely squatters' cabin in 1979. I came and went so much it was time to let someone else enjoy the tranquility of cabin life and zero rent. Years later when I went back, the land had been logged and the cabin flattened. I found the horseshoe that used to hang over the door, which I still have. Life in the cabin was very character building, such personal growth and changes. I left with the best of memories.

The Comox Valley has been very special for me. I travelled all over and feel very blessed to have landed here, home, in the Comox Valley. I'm still in gumboots, but having lived at times with a lot of snow, rain and gumboots are fine with me.

Follow the Tarvy Road

ROSEMARY VERNON
Arrived in 1973

I was feeling appreciation and relief on that vivid spring morning in 1976, the first day in our Comox Valley home. My husband, Ric, our young daughter, Alissa, and I had already strolled the six-acre field and explored some of the twenty-eight acres forested with many second-growth trees. From across the field, the six-room house looked weathered but charming. However, when that morning's eggs had rolled down the kitchen counter and smashed into the sink, we knew there was work to be done. This was the property we had fallen in love with in 1973 and where for three years we had been looking forward to putting down our family roots. I was appreciating how fortunate we were and feeling relieved that we were finally home.

I had first come to the Comox Valley in the late sixties, when teaching jobs were plentiful, and I was met with kindness. I valued growing up in Vancouver; however, like many young people, I wanted to discover what else there was to life.

At that time, young people from many countries were responding to the invitation to come to BC to teach. That sparked Ric and several of his friends to travel from Perth, Australia, to Campbell River; they too were embraced by the community. Ric caught the skiing bug, travelling every weekend up to Forbidden Plateau. Fortunately, mutual friends became matchmakers, and we were married in Courtenay in July 1970.

We intended to return to Australia, but first we wanted to see more of the world, and we moved to southern Peru to teach. That experience was rich and varied, and living in an international community broadened our views. Our horizons were also expanded by annual three-month trips to several continents. However, we also visited Vancouver Island to reconnect with those whose kindness we remembered, and on our third visit back, we jointly concluded to commit to this beautiful valley.

Clutching our worn copy of *Five Acres and Independence*, we added our names to the lengthy list of seekers at the local real estate office, who were not encouraging. Serendipitously, a few days later in the *Vancouver Sun* was a small ad for thirty-four acres, with an old house and some outbuildings, seven miles north of Courtenay, by private sale. When we called, the owners invited us to visit that afternoon, giving us directions that finished with "just follow the tarvy road to its end"—the first time we had heard that expression to describe a finished road surface—"then go a few driveways beyond." We strolled the property with our hosts, engaged by their honesty, sincerity and kindness. While the men toured the outbuildings and talked about the recent fencing, Lil and I located her beloved Jersey cow, Marie. Lil related searching in the woods for Marie and finding her in a sunny clearing, giving birth to her calf. To the right, a doe was licking her newborn fawn. I felt, *This is it!* Later, over tea and baked goodies, we agreed on the comfort we felt with each other; it was easy to make arrangements to purchase the property. What a whirlwind in such a short time! It was a mutual benefit that our new friends wanted to stay on as renters while we completed the next two years of our teaching contract.

The immense changes taking place in the world in the early seventies strongly emphasized the value of citizenship. Even though I was raised in Canada, I had been travelling on a British subject (residing in Canada) passport. Upon renewal of my passport in late 1974, I became a British subject residing in Peru. My Australian husband and I, along with our daughter, who was born in Peru in 1973 (a Peruvian citizen), began the worrying, lengthy and arduous process of immigrating to Canada. Ten months later, just as our Peruvian work visas were expiring, we boarded a flight to Vancouver, gratefully clutching our Canadian landed immigrant documents. In May 1976, three relieved and proud Canadian immigrants travelled the tarvy road (which had by now been extended well past our driveway) as residents, no longer visitors.

The summer months stretched ahead: time to plant a garden, think about what animals we would raise and assess the renovation of our house. Learning to garden was a whole new skill for me. We wanted to grow as much of our own food as possible, and I felt there was no time to waste. By mid-May, I had planted a garden plot with strawberries, lettuce, potatoes, radishes, carrots and beets. Then a severe overnight frost put me back to square one. A few days later, a knowledgeable neighbour told me that there was no point in planting before the long weekend in May, and if June was unpredictable, repeat plantings might be necessary. This was only the first of many humbling moments when I learned it was best to first ask questions of someone who was experienced!

Friends arrived one weekend in June with a bale of hay, eight laying hens and two bags of feed as their "welcome back to the Comox Valley." We were overjoyed to gather daily eggs, revelling in how superior they were to store-bought eggs. The hens looked so content scratching away at piles of leaves and grass clippings. We also welcomed two stately Peking ducks, but would soon learn that free-range birds make an easy meal for predators. With no ducks and only four hens remaining by midsummer, we vowed to learn more and become vigilant.

Beginning renovations was challenging. A new septic system was required, so we tackled that first. A builder friend who inspected our house concluded that it "had good bones" and was worth renovating. However, it would need a foundation, as it had spent its life resting on rocks and logs. Once again, several neighbours came to the rescue, offering to walk us through the process, from jacking up the house, pouring footings and then laying the foundation.

Like so many unique pockets around the Comox Valley, Merville had been settled by returning World War One veterans who had taken the offer of fifty acres and the materials to build a home. We discovered our

We soon discovered that the septic system for our new house was a forty-five-gallon drum and that the house was on a foundation of rotting logs! Photo Ric Vernon

thirty-four acres and the sixteen acres next door had been one parcel prior to the just-established Agricultural Land Reserve. In the early twenties, a war veteran and his family had settled there and built the existing house. A family of eight had lived there, which put an end to our complaints of not having enough room for a family of three! Over time, previous residents stopped by to tell us their stories and to see what we had done to "the old place." My favourite was the elderly gentleman who, as a nine-year-old, had helped his father hand-dig the nineteen-foot well at the back of the house. The well was still in use and the quality of the water was superb. He told us that life in that tiny community had centred around helping each other, sharing resources and simple entertainment.

I reflected on that conversation often. So many of us in that era were do-it-yourselfers, determined to renovate or build our own homes and work our land. Few of us had the skills and the resources to be successful on our own. Ric and I relied a great deal on the generosity of our neighbours, who so willingly supported us with their time and expertise. We and other new-comer friends were learning by doing, sometimes from mistakes. In one case, Ric and I wanted to open up several of the rooms in our house to create an open plan. The very solid interior walls were tongue-and-groove fir shiplap on both sides of the two-by-fours. Ric and a friend used their chainsaws to

Break time from the demanding role of gofer. Soon my skill set increased to not only fetching tools, but also knowing how to use them! Photo Ric Vernon

expedite the process. Fortunately, there was no electrical wiring and they had taken the time to identify the bearing walls! Another time, we had a gathering to install our wood stove. All went according to plan until the friend who had been checking the pipe going through the attic slipped off the rafter and came through the ceiling. What a relief he wasn't injured! The first fire was lit and the home-brewed beer was passed around as we celebrated that relief and the group's success.

We also all wanted to support ourselves from the land as much as possible. Many of us had grown up in cities, Ric and me included. After my early attempts at gardening, I often referred to our neighbour's advice to work with soil conditions and weather patterns, and not to be discouraged by the hungry deer. Despite the advice, I wasn't particularly successful at gardening, but I did discover by trial and error which plants worked best. Other newly arrived friends were also learning. The world of canning, pickling, dehydrating and freezing had opened to us. It was fun to gather together, set up activities for the children, put on the music and work on the project of the day. Our tongues moved as quickly as our fingers as we sorted, chopped, mixed and adjusted recipes. We agreed on the satisfaction we felt and that we were getting to know each other better by working together.

We also acquired livestock. Despite our unhappy beginning with poultry, we were keen to try again with a flock of twenty to thirty birds. We found it difficult to cull the hens that were too old to lay eggs, but we learned to sort and butcher humanely, sharing the meat with our helpers. Incubating and hatching our own chicks was not very successful, but the second time around, we heeded the suggestion that we attend the local Saturday auction.

Before our arrival, the open pasture had always had a small herd of grazing cows. A neighbour brought his cows down for a couple of months. Soon, we couldn't imagine there being no cows, so we acquired Rita and her calf, Rosa. With three friends, we purchased a quarter share in a Shorthorn bull, a magnificent creature with a gleam in his eyes who ensured that our herd grew in numbers. Cows in the field were a great joy, especially when the calves were born, cared for and named by family. Eventually, we enjoyed the company of twelve cows in the field, and we had no beef in the freezer!

We also acquired two piglets, who were adorable, but we didn't get as attached to them, perhaps because of their generic names, Pig One and Pig Two, and because they grew bigger, uglier and hungrier as time went on. It became impossible to consider keeping them beyond their "ready to go to market" date. Fortunately, Gunter Bros. Meat Co. Ltd. provided wonderful service, allowing us to wave goodbye after six months and soon say hello to pork wrapped in brown paper, which we shared with appreciative friends and family. To that we added home-prepared gifts of headcheese (brawn) and liverwurst, which I learned to make while working with our next-door neighbour's mom.

While we were making additions to our home and livestock, we were also making additions to our family. In 1977 Ric, Alissa and I welcomed Hayley, rounding off the decade with the arrival of Alissa and Hayley's brother, Roger. Unlike what I remembered of growing up in the city, our children couldn't just hop the fence to visit their friends. Soon after our arrival, several of us decided to have a gathering every Wednesday afternoon, rotating weekly from home to home. Our guidelines for hosting were: keep it casual, no need to clean house, serve only coffee or tea for the moms, with a snack for the kids, and encourage as much outside play as possible. The children came to know each other so well that being together was a highlight of their week. I too really looked forward to those Wednesday afternoons. We would bring our ongoing projects, and I have vivid memories of stories, laughter, occasional tears and many hugs. These very special

The house is almost at completion, produce exceeds expectations, Alissa and Hayley are thriving on rural life and, three days later, Roger was born! Photo Ric Vernon

afternoons gradually faded away as our youngest children headed off to school and we slipped into the next phase of life.

Alissa rode her first school bus to kindergarten at Tsolum Elementary School in September 1978. Over the next eight years, she would be followed in turn by her siblings. This wonderful rural school was the heart of the Tsolum/Merville community, and during the time our children attended, the entire community gathered together to celebrate its sixtieth anniversary, bringing back memories for long-time residents and bringing its rich community history alive for those of us who were newcomers. Many of us were eager to participate at the school and to volunteer in our children's classrooms, and several of us set up our own informal roster to care for each other's younger children. Also, during the late seventies and early eighties, parent consultative committees were being introduced into schools, encouraging parent involvement in school planning and decision-making, added to the traditional role of fundraising. I eagerly joined other interested parents who wanted to work in partnership with school staff to support all the children.

I also enjoyed volunteering with the local 4-H club. A friend asked if I would like to be her assistant leader in the 4-H home arts program. This was interesting, but the real eye-opener came when all the clubs, mostly focussed on raising animals, gathered together to present and share what had been learned. I was in awe of how much those young people accomplished each year and how their all-around development was encouraged and supported by that long-established organization and its local volunteer leaders.

During the seventies, the door was inching open for women to make choices in how they wanted to live their lives. It was also a time when many couples were talking about what worked best for them. In early 1978, it was time for us to review life. Ric was thoroughly enjoying teaching at Black Creek Elementary, another rural school at the centre of its community. I was thrilled he was gaining enlightened ideas on life from fellow female staff. The evening before the first staff luncheon, he informed me that he and the other men had to choose and prepare their own dishes to contribute, with no involvement from their wives. Who was going to argue with that?

While on maternity leave, I had started to think about returning to teaching. I clearly remembered the challenge of finding reliable care for Alissa. As we would soon need care for two young children, Ric supported my decision to not return to teaching at that time. Other young parents, most having no nearby family support, who were trying to work, doing contract work or thinking about returning to work, had the same predicament.

We all agreed that we wanted our children to feel the support of other adults and the friendship of children of all ages. Our home became a haven for my friends' children, and I was greatly pleased to be there for those children and parents.

In the spring of 1978, we visited our friends Denis and Peggy Kabush at their cottage on Hornby Island. Peggy and I had been high school classmates and had recently reconnected. Denis and Ric were teaching together at Black Creek. We were really enthralled by their stories of summers spent enjoying the outstanding beauty of the island and were impressed by its relative proximity to our home. We took the big step of buying a piece of that heaven, just down the road from them. Memorable family summers of camping, swimming and beachcombing stretched out ahead of us.

In the seventies, as in earlier times, we made our own simple entertainment. Couples, families, friends and neighbours acquired skills, gathered firewood and brought in hay together. All year long, we took turns hosting regular potlucks, on a theme or not. We had singalongs at the piano and with guitars. We barbecued in the summer and fondued in the winter. We learned how to make beer and wine, celebrating with wonderful tasting parties. We gathered together on each other's ponds to skate in the winter. In the summer, we walked down the shady paths to cool off at the swimming hole where the Tsolum River meets Dove Creek. We bundled up the kids, made popcorn and headed to the Stardust Drive-In. We made snow forts and sledded on Forbidden Plateau. At the Renaissance Fair, we ate scrumptious food, sang along with musicians and bought beautiful artisan works. We danced to records, we danced to eight-track tapes and we danced to live music. We danced in our living rooms, we danced in our fields and we danced at the community halls. Sometimes, gumboots were involved!

In 2005 camping on Hornby Island became living on Hornby Island, where we are enjoying our retirement years. Our three children and their families eventually settled in the Comox Valley. Our daughter and her family now own the family property. Every summer, we look forward to returning to the swimming hole, which is now part of Tsolum Spirit Regional Park. We eagerly anticipate meeting up with many friends from the area at the annual wreath-making party. I am so appreciative that we arrived there many years ago, following the tarvy road.

Journey to the River

JACKIE SANDIFORD
Arrived in 1973

On April Fool's Day 1974 (we considered it an auspicious day), ten of us signed the papers as tenants in common, buying 102.5 acres of land in Merville at the foot of Mount Washington on the banks of the Tsolum River. We continued to call our new home the Hermitage, a name inherited from the Catholic monks who had originally retreated there. I was thirty-three that year. According to the *I Ching*, thirty-three is "retreat," and for me it was a real retreat from my Vancouver city life. Often, I went to Courtenay only twice a week, and there were times when I lived like a hermit. I have a theory that all of us went through a hermitic period at some time while living there.

Judy, my close friend, and I had been looking for land for two years to better raise our children, get out of the city and get "back to the land." When we first looked at the Hermitage, I said, "Not perfect, but it will do." Later that summer, lying in the sun by the river, we laughed about that "not perfect" comment, as at that moment it seemed perfect. In the early years, many of us would meet at the swimming hole in the late afternoon and sunbathe and swim, until the trees grew too tall and the beach too shaded. Coming to the Hermitage felt a lot like coming home, and that we are still there forty-five years later says how much it is our home.

Judy moved into the longhouse, originally a bunkhouse for a logging operation, with her four children, and I moved into the adjacent two-room cabin with my daughter. We came and went across the river on a suspension bridge that had been built by the monks, until it was washed away by the floods. My daughter reminded me of how she had to straddle the remaining cables with only a guide wire for support to get to school and to visit her friends. After three years, I moved across the creek to another part of the land.

Approaching the Hermitage, crossing the Tsolum River on the swinging bridge, with my cabin and part of the longhouse visible in the meadow.

We all had different expectations about moving back to and sharing the land. The reality was that we all had our hands full just keeping the wood stoves going and our own lives on track. Forty-five years later, some of us are close friends, all are good neighbours and we are still functioning as tenants in common with few rules.

The first years were spent homesteading. I learned how to build—first a woodshed of slabs, a by-product of sawmilling consisting of the edges, bark still on, crude and cheap. I was given a chainsaw and filled my new woodshed with five cords of firewood. We lived in the two-room cabin, which was a little too small for me and a budding teenager, so I built an attic bedroom and then a gypsy caravan for my daughter. I learned by using scrounged wood and advice from friends. I figured it was a lot like sewing, but the materials are more unwieldy and less forgiving.

I have been living off the grid on my own since 1977, when I moved out of the cabin and into a small, six-sided building, one of the hermits' original cells. My friend and construction adviser, Gordon, offered me an unfinished ten-by-fourteen-foot shed that was sitting on his farm in Comox. We moved it to Merville on his hay wagon, pulled by his tractor, and I finished attaching it to the hexagon during the first snowfall. After another big flood, it had to be moved again, this time to higher ground farther away from the river, as I now realized that half of our land is flood plain. Two friends raised it six feet, constructed the foundation and framed an addition, which I finished during the following year by installing doors, windows and recycled fir flooring, and putting up walls, ceilings and beds, all done with hand tools. This was the era of pink insulation and plastic: so many of us have lived with this aesthetic, often for longer than a year. After I finished this project, I was done with building. However, every year five cords of firewood had to be bucked up, hauled and split. I quit using my chainsaw in my sixties.

I also learned how to garden by doing. There was a fenced plot next to my first house. What a pleasure it was to bring back an easily restored garden. When I moved, my next garden was an unfenced bed of thistles. I thought I could just share with the deer; however, they did not understand sharing and ate it all. Now my clearing has a deer fence that is attached to handy trees, with a large perennial flower garden and a productive veggie area. I have not enjoyed shooting the rabbits that migrated here, but they are also not good at sharing. But I love cutting the lawn with my push mower, which I call "pumping iron," and watering using my wheelbarrow, nominally "running water." Even without running water, gardening remains one of my greatest pleasures.

A year before we moved to the Comox Valley, I began to learn tai chi, and I was fortunate to have my teacher come for visits and continued instruction for the first few years. Then I hitchhiked once a month to Vancouver to study with a tai chi master who eventually came to the valley and taught weekly classes for a few years. By this time I was committed to my daily practice, which continues to this day: tai chi, a stick form and qigong. We managed to help Henry and his family immigrate to Comox from Taiwan, and I studied with him for fifteen years and now with his wife, Ivy. I also taught tai chi at the Lewis and Filberg centres for some of this period. I consider it a lifetime study, and I practise daily for about two hours in a lovely spot where the creek and the river meet. When I am done, I sit up against a very large old blue spruce tree, return the energy to the earth and send it as healing energy to my friends.

Throughout this time, my relationship with the river and the land continued to deepen, root and grow. I carried and drank my water from it, lay in the sun beside it, swam in it, watched its wildlife as I did my dishes, ate at a table beside it daily. When it floods my woodshed and the whole clearing, I am submerged in it! The river became a part of my consciousness; my connection, love and respect for it deepens. Because I am off the grid and

Practicing tai chi (Snake Creeps Down) in the clearing by Wolfe Creek and the Tsolum River.

have grown to appreciate the natural sounds, I prefer to listen to the quiet around me. It lets my mind expand and open to a level that feeds my spirit. The land and all the beings I share it with are an integral part of myself.

I never thought I would become an environmentalist until I saw my first clear-cut, and then there was no ignoring the devastation. My environmental activism began when TimberWest wanted to spray herbicides on a cutblock, recently logged, adjacent to the creek that provided our drinking water. After unsuccessful talks, we erected a half-day blockade. Then I phoned their head office and said, "We really do not want to do this; how can we resolve this situation so it works for all of us?" We ended up applying for and running a job-training program funded by a grant from the government to clear the block manually, thus avoiding the spraying, and continued at the request of TimberWest for a second year. This was the beginning of years of trying to work with this logging corporation on issues that impacted our community. Our most successful negotiation with them was identifying and keeping the trees bordering the Tsolum River, which should not be cut because they shade and shelter the river. Their intention was to trade the strip along the river, ceding it to the regional district for a park, but only after logging it. The park now exists, trees intact, as an extension of the One Spot Trail. When our land and water were mistreated and destroyed in the name of progress and profit, I felt no choice but to take action.

In 1990, while teaching English in Japan for four months, I had an epiphany about water. I came home with the conviction that water is our biggest issue. I attended a conference about water, organized by Chris of the Department of Fisheries and Oceans. Inspired by his vision, I was involved in helping to create Project Watershed and later the Watershed Assembly, for which I worked as the secretary for four years. The assembly functioned on the premise that if enough people were concerned about an issue, a group would be formed that included all parties with an interest (that is, the stakeholders) to address the issue. When needed, we provided a facilitator. Out of the assembly came the Comox Valley Land Trust, the Tsolum River Restoration Society and other citizen groups, some still going strong.

Our Tsolum River had been polluted by a fly-by-night copper-mining operation and was declared a dead river in the eighties. Through the assembly, we formed the Tsolum River Task Force, and I was employed as the assistant coordinator for a few years. We tried to initiate repair to the mine site, involving all levels of government and private interests. When this initiative failed, the Tsolum River Restoration Society was formed, and it included many of the same citizens who had served on the task force. I served on the board of the society until the Tsolum was declared a recovered river. It has now had large runs of pink salmon (sixty thousand) in 2015 and 2017. There are success stories!

These days I live with the river and the land, practice my tai chi, garden, am a MervilleGrandMother, enjoy my family, friends and community, and travel to Mexico for five or six months every winter. I live below the poverty line and deeply appreciate my life and the Tsolum River.

I Took the Scenic Routes

MONIKA TERFLOTH
Arrived in 1973

There was never a question that I would leave home right after finishing high school. In my family, when we graduated from high school we usually received one of those plastic luggage sets with the chrome snaps. My older sister got a red one with a matching cosmetics case the size of breadbox. As I recall, mine was blue. I had always envied my school friends who got to go on exotic summer vacations to the Okanagan and such places. Some had even seen the ocean. Our family didn't have the money for that sort of thing. Our house was far too small for seven growing teenagers, and I, as second oldest, knew it was time to leave.

My parents left Germany after the war, disembarking in Halifax and taking the train westward to settle among other German immigrants in a small town in northern Saskatchewan. My father, though a cabinetmaker, was really also a rebel and an activist. He had vowed never to stop learning and believed there was more than one way to get an education. I was encouraged, but at seventeen, I had no real direction in mind other than out. So, he took the liberty of registering me at the University of Saskatchewan while I had my back turned for just a second that summer after high school. Such audacity! I went anyway. Besides, my sister was going—but jeez, our dad was going too! He had returned to school a few years before and needed to finish his psychology degree. He grew his hair, smoked pot and marched in protests alongside us, and pretty much set the stage for what was to follow. It was at the U of S in 1971 that I met Randy, a long-haired hippie with a broad grin who became the love of my life. It took me only another five years to figure that out.

The first year at university was a bust. I rarely went to class, partied far too much and almost flunked out. When, in May the following year, Randy announced he was heading out west with his friend Barry and asked if I would like to come, I didn't take a moment to decide. Encouraged by my family, I traded my blue plastic suitcase for a Trapper Nelson pack and emptied my bank account of the two hundred dollars I had saved, certain it was enough to last the summer. For transport, Randy had found an old home-delivery milk van named Metro. That van was something! Metro was a golden-tan colour, generously toasted with rust around the edges and fittingly shaped like a loaf of bread, still smelling faintly of sour milk.

We threw in our sleeping bags, a few scrounged cook pots and an old blue canvas tent. We planned to live off the land, and we had Euell Gibbons' *Stalking the Wild Asparagus* and the *Whole Earth Catalogue* for guidance. It wasn't a problem that Metro had only one seat, the driver's. We simply placed two collapsible lawn chairs in the cab for Barry and me. They were cheap and would be versatile. We swooped, unfastened, along the winding highway through the Rockies. We purposely left the sliding door open to make the curves more exhilarating! I was terrified at first and never once sat in the lawn chair next to the door. We headed west on a May morning, leaving the blue Saskatchewan sky, the mosquitoes and the dust storms behind.

We poked along through the Okanagan and spent a few days at Stanley Park before heading for Vancouver Island. Though by now I had seen the ocean, I was unprepared for the jaw-dropping expanse of the blue Pacific that blinded us as we rounded a corner at the top of a cliff on the

We paid regular visits to our trusty van, Metro, who wasn't allowed to camp with us farther down the beach.

approach to Long Beach. That scene is forever imprinted on my mind. We drove Metro right to the water's edge. One could in those days. The month of June was spent living under a black plastic tarp stretched between the logs. We feasted on salmon and salmonberries and tiny wild strawberries. We made cattail-pollen pancakes and pulled barnacles off rocks. For store-bought necessities, we collected bottles and turned them in for cash. By the time July rolled around, it was time to move along. We'd heard about Denman Island from other travellers, and that it was possible to camp at Fillongley Park right by the ocean. It sounded perfect. So, Metro hauled us back eastward over Mount Arrowsmith, took a left at Qualicum Beach and headed north up the lovely, twisty, narrow Old Island Highway, past broken-down barns and through small towns with silly names like Bowser and Fanny Bay, to arrive at the ferry dock for Denman Island.

That first hill coming off the ferry at Denman was a bit of a struggle for Metro, and the second hill was nearly as bad. We pulled in at Fillongley Park to discover the campground virtually empty. There, in a choice spot with our backs to a forest of monumental trees, at the base of the trail leading up to the meadows, we parked. We stayed for four months. It was a small thing to hike north up the beach to where a freshwater spring spouted from a ferny embankment: cold, clear water and the ideal place for a private bath or a laundry day. We felt we had landed in paradise.

We gathered oysters, dug for clams and fished for ocean perch at the wharf. We collected glasswort and seaweed for greens. Parksman Pete ran the campground, and from time to time he'd give us odd jobs to help stretch the dollars. There was a slope in front of his house that was choked with daffodil bulbs. This Saskatchewan girl had never seen a daffodil bulb and certainly didn't know that they would fatten and multiply until they would choke each other! It was my mission to save them from themselves. Wheelbarrow load after wheelbarrow load of daffodil bulbs came up; it was gruelling work in the heat of the summer. It was my first foray into gardening, and I loved it. I still do. Chickadee Lake was perfect for cooling off afterward, and skinny-dipping was pretty much a requirement. Besides, we weren't bashful.

We spent evenings talking by the campfire with other travellers, many of whom were draft dodgers and Vietnam War resisters from the US. More conventional folks would also drop by. They'd arrive in fully equipped campers, often with ovens. An oven was pure luxury to us. They were happy to share and make up a pie and bake it if we would pick the huckleberries. Sometimes they would change their minds about us, sometimes not.

Every couple of weeks, a trip into Courtenay was necessary. We'd pick up any hitchhikers and together collect the freebies we'd learned about. At the vegetable packing plant that used to sit behind the Arbutus Hotel, we were allowed to scavenge for rejected potatoes and carrots, and the "just barely out of date" dairy products were left out on the loading dock behind the milk plant for anyone to pick up. Fruit was ripening on the island and easy to come by. Because Metro once needed a break before climbing the second long hill on Denman Island, we found the most succulent yellow plums on a tree at the base of that hill. And so it was for the rest of that summer and fall, gleaning what we could. As November approached, we were finally broke, the weather was getting cold and wet and it seemed sensible to come inside. A solid roof was very appealing. But there would be rent to pay, and Metro needed a U-joint. Clearly it was time to find steady work.

As soon as we cut Randy's long, bushy hair, he found work picking oysters, his shifts determined by the tides. Barry's waist-length golden hair, which he brushed until it shone, was another matter. He refused to cut it. Of course. So ultimately he took over the household tasks. With at least one of us having work, we set out to find a place to live. Nobody would rent to us: a couple living in sin and with a long-haired friend. In the end we lied. Barry tucked his golden locks under a cap, Randy and I pretended to be brother and sister, and a leaky, drafty house along the highway in Fanny Bay became our home that winter. It suited us just fine; besides, Metro was tired.

At last I also found work. It was a job entirely unsuited for me, I thought. I was fitted with a neon-green polyester uniform and began to stock shelves and run the till at a discount store on Fifth Street in Courtenay. It's no longer there, but then neither are many of the shops that lined Fifth Street and made it the hub of the community at that time. Getting to work in Courtenay from Fanny Bay was complicated. With Metro on sabbatical, I would stand on the side of the highway opposite our house and hitchhike into Courtenay each morning and return the same way each evening. I learned about black ice, a coastal hazard that I had never before heard of, tricky stuff that could catch one unaware.

We would often spend an evening at the Fanny Bay Inn just down the road from our place. The pub was full of oyster shuckers and fishermen smelling of sea water and salt. Many of them lived along the Island Highway as far as Union Bay and were part of families that had been there for generations. They would bring smoked eulachons or oysters to the pub and pass them around. It didn't matter if they knew you or not. These folks grumbled quietly about the changes happening in the area. There were a lot of hippies moving in and homesteading farther north. We weren't a part of that. Yet.

The days shortened, the rain pelted and the fog smothered. The house was damp, and even the moss crept in. I longed for the prairies, the brilliant blue sky and crackling white snow. The only brilliance in my life came under fluorescent lights as I stacked bottles of bubble bath, shampoo and rinses that promised to turn white hair a delightful shade of pink, lavender or blue. I worked with Hazel, Helen and Gwen. They were conventional women, not really my type. Hazel was a Lucille Ball look-alike with a husband in the air force, Helen was motherly and had grown children, and Gwen still lived with her parents. We didn't seem to have a lot in common, but I believe those women saved me during a difficult time.

I had been on the birth control pill for six months, since May, when I had walked into a doctor's office and walked out with a round plastic dispenser of Ovral. As liberating as the birth control pill was for women, it could be hell at the same time. It would be many more years before it was determined that effective dosages were a fraction of what was routinely prescribed back then. I had put on weight despite a diet of seafood and rice. I was moody, if not outright depressed. I couldn't sleep, and I would stand out in the blue-black mornings on the side of the road, waiting for headlights to round the corner, feeling that life was pointless. I felt like I was on black ice of a different kind.

The discount store, with all its garishness, was safe. I believe these women sensed I was vulnerable. They would never mention it if I came in dripping wet and cold and late for work. A cigarette and a Nescafé were waiting for me in the back room, or they would take me to lunch at the Chinese café down the street. They guessed that Randy wasn't my brother and didn't say a word. They were steady and caring and necessary to my survival.

By April, even the sunshine and the emerging primroses and daffodils couldn't bring me around. I guessed it was time to go back home. The tipping point might have been an oyster loaf. I had come home from work and Randy had dinner ready. He presented a baked loaf of his own creation, made of ground oysters, bread crumbs and corn kernels stuck together with egg. I believe the first mouthful of that green-streaked loaf confirmed what I already knew. It was time to go back home to Saskatchewan.

Being away from Randy meant I could quit the pill, and before the Saskatchewan summer was over, I felt like myself again. It wasn't until much later, perhaps even years later, that I made the connection and assigned the blame. It could have been worse, and for many women it was.

Soon, however, a longing for the ocean kicked in. I missed its smell. I missed its roar. I missed the sound of the gulls, and I missed sitting on its rocky edge. There was word of work in the fish canneries up in Prince Rupert. Once again, I hardly took a second to decide to head up there. I spent a couple of years during the mid-seventies working in Prince Rupert. In the off-season, I hitchhiked as far north as Whitehorse and back down the Alaska Highway, often hitching back to Prince Rupert on the "Highway of Tears." I was one of the lucky ones. I travelled south to Central America, and I hitched back and forth on Highway 1 to Saskatchewan for family gatherings. All this time the Comox Valley remained my touchstone. It was where I met friends who lived elsewhere. They were among those who swarmed out of the cities and off the Gulf Islands to come to the Renaissance Fair each summer. The fall might bring them back again to harvest magic mushrooms. Randy was still on the Island, so we'd reconnect and scout for land and envy friends who had already found a place. Soon, we had a kid on the way. We then decided we ought to stick together rather than gallivanting off in opposite directions as we had been doing (and are still known to do).

Because land prices were out of our reach at the time, we decided to live in a trailer park on the north end of Vancouver Island, work hard and save every penny until we could afford a homestead in the Comox Valley. Life in a logging town was a challenge! But close friends had moved up with us, and together we began to learn about building community. So much needed to be done for families there. We worked hard to start the first pre-school and create an artisan fair. We brought facilitators up from Courtenay to help get a women's group started, and we arranged bulk deliveries of organic fruit and nuts.

During those three years, we came to the Comox Valley every chance we could to look for land, and to stock up at Edible Island. We were certain the valley would eventually become our home. At last, with the help of friends, we found our home in Merville in a neighbourhood of other young families, and there we raised our three children. Randy and I still live in Merville, and it remains a precious place. We plan to stay, but if we leave it certainly won't be far.

At the same time that I was fully embracing motherhood, I wanted to learn something new (truly my father's daughter), and I also wanted financial independence. I wanted to go back to school. So with the support of family and friends, I began nursing school when my youngest child was three. Women's reproductive health had always interested me, and I secretly

Fall harvest. Here we demonstrate various postures for the seeking and collection of magic mushrooms.

held a hilarious vision of myself as a midwife on horseback, galloping off to help a woman in labour. I wanted to combine my homestead life with other vital work. That vision soon dissipated as I stepped from a life of knitting sweaters, breastfeeding babies and baking bread to go back under blazing fluorescent lights to work among women. I loved it. The hospitals were full of amazing women working in conventional roles and doing amazing things. It was exactly what I wanted.

My dad finally came to visit after we'd lived in Merville for several years. He always got riled if anyone said anything negative about Saskatchewan. He believed Saskatchewan was the most beautiful place on earth. After showing him around the valley, after collecting oysters on the beach, after he'd sensed the vitality in my community, he leaned over to say in a whisper, "I think your mom and I may have got off the train too soon." I'm not sorry they did, for he loved Saskatchewan and so do I, even still. But the Comox Valley is my home and my community. I am grateful for it.

How Did I Get Here?

SUSAN SANDLAND
Arrived in 1974

How did I get here—to the Comox Valley? Like many, I took a circuitous route. After completing a bachelor of arts degree at Macalester College in Saint Paul, Minnesota, I came to Canada, along with many students who were fleeing the draft and the Vietnam War. The year was 1968. I went to Toronto, taught in the education clinic at the Ontario Institute for Studies in Education and received my teaching degree at Toronto Teachers' College. In 1972 my partner and I came west to Victoria, BC. As a young child I had lived on Whidbey Island with my family while my father was in the US Navy fighting in the Korean War. I loved the island and the ocean, and I had a great desire to return to the West Coast, this time of Canada. In Victoria I worked as a child-care worker at a treatment centre for children called Seven Oaks, and I built a pan-abode cabin in Saanich.

I am the granddaughter of Swedish farmers in Minnesota and, even though I grew up in a big city, I loved spending time on the farm with my grandparents and summers at a lake cabin. I felt a calling to country life, as did many of my contemporaries. So, I spent the summer of 1974, this time with a new partner and a camperized old school bus, travelling around BC looking for a new home in the country. We loved the Kootenays, but the call of the ocean was very strong. We returned to Vancouver Island. By this time, I was pregnant and wanted a location with no smells of pulp and paper mills—a rural environment without air pollution in which to raise a family. The Comox Valley, also known as the Land of Plenty, fit the criteria and had an abundance of agricultural land.

It was coming on to winter and I didn't relish the thought of having a baby in the school bus. We found an unfinished house built by a fisherman, Peter, who was also building his boat, the Beowulf, at the same time. Something had to go as Peter couldn't continue with both projects; so, he

This is the house that Susan built on the Tsolum River in Merville. Photo Susan Sand-land

sold us the house located on Forbidden Plateau Road. That winter was cold and snowy and the baby, Erin, decided that being born in the middle of a snowstorm was a great way to start life! We drove to the hospital through unplowed roads and three feet of fresh snow. Fortunately, we had an old Volvo and could plow our own way.

In the spring we got two pigs, to start clearing land for a veggie garden, and milking goats. Our bantam chickens roosted in the trees and hid their nests, arriving later with a clutch of babies.

The two pregnant goats, Ma and Talulah, were most entertaining. We had Dutch doors (made by Peter the Dutchman) where the top half could be open and the bottom half closed. Ma and Talulah were frequently seen peering through the open top half of the door, watching the goings-on of the family and wanting to join in, I am sure. There was a pantry under the stairway and sometimes I would find two heads poking their way through the trap door: the goats had found their way into the crawl space under the house. They gave us lots of milk, as their breed is known to be the dairy producers of the goat world. We made cheese and yogurt by the gallons. Every year they presented us with kids. While I was milking Ma and Talu-lah, two-year-old Erin could often be found playing with the goat kids in the goat pen. She would fall over, then try to right herself again by getting on

Two-year-old Erin with her playmates, the goat kids. Photo Susan Sandland

hands and feet with her bum in the air. Well, you can imagine what a perfect target she made for the kid goats! They were relentless! "Hey, this is a fun game!" they said. Pretty soon I would hear Erin call, "Maaaaa," sounding almost like a goat herself, and then it was Mom to the rescue! When I would hear cars stop on the road in front of the house, I knew instinctively what was happening: my daughter, with white and curly angel hair and wearing gumboots, was prancing and dancing on the road with the five white goats. She was just one of the kids!

Because of my Scandinavian background I was interested in fibres, namely spinning fleece, dying hand-spun yarn and weaving. One year I tried to earn a living at my weaving. I had a forty-six-inch Leclerc loom from Quebec and an Ashford spinning wheel from New Zealand. I made blankets, cushions, clothing, vests, jerkins and fabric lengths—everything sold, but I made only five cents an hour. Definitely not enough to live on! I did, however, help found the Woolgatherers, a spinning and weaving guild, which is still active today.

When we no longer had goats, the Glacier Fed Food Co-op moved into the goat shed. This co-op was connected to the Fed-Up Food Co-op in Vancouver. Later came the Edible Island co-op, still a thriving business today over thirty-seven years later.

Back in 1974, while I was still living in the school bus, a friend, Shirley, and I happened upon a property in Merville on the Tsolum River. It was part of an old subdivision from 1913 in the Headquarters Townsite. As we walked along the river trail and through the natural meadow, we imagined a group of people coming to live on this land, building houses in the trees and leaving the meadow and flood plain in its natural state as a wildlife corridor. This was a vision which was to come to fruition four years later. In 1977 this same land, of about 160 acres, came on the market. It was located across the river from the Hermitage (100 acres owned by a group of people). Judy, of the Hermitage, offered to buy it from Gordon and his son Smokey, surveyors and owners of the land, if she could have a year to find a group of people to do the actual purchase. Thus began a journey of finding those interested and committed people. I became one of those people from the very beginning. (My daughter's father had left our family and we needed to sell the Forbidden Plateau Road house.) It was a long process of meetings with the owners of the land—a revolving door of people coming and going. It took a year for the final solid group of committed people to put in our offers and have them accepted. The parcels we bought, between two and six acres each, had been subdivided in 1913, so we each had separate titles to our acreages. At our final meeting, we decided we wanted to buy the two meadow parcels as a group. Smokey was not in favour of having nineteen people as the purchasers, with him and his father holding the mortgage. He felt it was too risky.

Gordon decided to take three-year-old Erin for a walk in the meadow while the group discussed the situation in private. We wanted the meadow for neighbourhood parkland and to provide river access for those who had none. When Gordon and Erin (our little angel in the mix) returned, Gordon agreed to let us buy what became known as the River Common (only one six-acre piece out of a possible ten acres). We invited Gordon to keep a share (there were eleven legal shares total) and we all steadfastly paid the mortgage off in about ten years.

In the summer of 1978, I started building my house with the help of Erin's father and his new girlfriend. Not an easy situation to say the least, but we made it work; we all wanted Erin and her mother to have a home. We built with recycled materials from houses in Victoria that were being torn down. We made leaded and stained-glass windows. After we hand-split the shakes, my new neighbours helped nail the shake roof.

All this was done with hand tools and a gas generator, as there was no hydro on Railway Avenue, our new street. It took another year and ten committed owners to get a Rural Electrification Grant before we got electricity. I made the double front doors from tongue-and-groove cedar and my friend Colin hand-forged the hinges. The front steps were granite headstones we found in the bush at one of Piercy's Funeral Home's quarries. In the seventies, many of us built our own homes in the country—and they were true creations! Most of us were not trained or qualified carpenters, but my completed house did pass inspection after Erin's grandfather, a civil engineer, made technical drawings.

Many are the memories of dances at the Merville Hall. We would dance to the lively, friendly tunes of Pied Pumpkin and, later, Pied Pear. They were family affairs, with babies sleeping in baskets under the tables and toddlers and youngsters alike kicking up their gumboots with their families to all the familiar tunes of the day! As Leonard Cohen so eloquently wrote, "Dance me to the end of love." And we did! But I didn't follow his other verse, "So don't forget who's taking you home, and in whose arms you're gonna be…" I met Oliver at one of the Pied Pear dances and said to him that infamous line, "Don't I know you from somewhere?" We talked for hours, going back into the history of our lives, back to college days at Macalester College where we were both students in the sixties and how, after graduating, he became a draft dodger. I took Oliver home and there he stayed. We raised a family and had a son, Andrew, together. "…So darling, save the last dance for me!"

With my teaching degree in hand, I became a primary teacher for some thirty years, teaching mainly in our rural neighbourhood at Tsolum Elementary School. I also found a lifelong passion and lifesaver in yoga practice and philosophy. After becoming a yoga teacher, I opened a studio, which I named Tsolum Spirit Yoga.

While I reflect upon the place where I have lived for the last forty years, I am awestruck and full of gratitude for the land, the river and the people who have lived here, past and present. We raised our children in a village and community setting where everyone contributed to the children's growth and upbringing. The adults in our neighbourhood alone are major contributors to the Comox Valley as a whole; some examples are: a school board trustee, the regional district director, founders of the World Community Development Education Society, members of the Fertile Ground non-profit society, a sculpture and video artist, a veterinarian, environmentalists, teachers, accountant, miners, a tech engineer, anthropologists, tree planters, health workers, an oyster grower, musicians, ferry workers and a secretary.

And, of course, there is the River Common on the Tsolum River, where children learn to swim, we walk our dogs, and everyone celebrates the seasons and observes the cycles of nature, like during the annual western toad migration and salmon spawning. Our neighbours, who work with the Tsolum River Restoration Society, have been instrumental in returning the river to a viable spawning river. We have an annual winter solstice celebration with a huge bonfire, a pageant—with a chorus telling the story, the characters Winter and Summer created with large masks on standards—circle dancing and singing, and we light little boats with candles, making wishes for the year and sending them down the river. It is a magical celebration of the changing of the seasons. We also have a maypole for Beltane.

The River Common has been our park and gathering place. Just recently, we donated the six acres of land as a park to the Comox Valley Land Trust Society. They in turn are leasing the park to the Regional District for ninety-nine years, with renewal available afterwards for another ninety-nine years.

And so, I feel blessed to have found this place in the Comox Valley, a Land of Plenty.

This is how I got here:

I got here through the gate.

I got here through a summer of searching, through a fall of expecting and through a winter of birthing.

I got here by opening my heart, my body, my spine and my third eye.

I got here by choices and choosing, by teaching and being taught, by creating and destroying, by dancing and sitting quietly, by fire and phoenix rising, by trial and error, in darkness and in light.

I got here by everyone I have ever loved and everyone who has ever loved me.

I got here by grace, especially by grace and breathing one breath at a time.

And that is how I got to this place, at this time, with the turning of the tides and the seasons.

This story is dedicated to my daughter, Erin Sandland-Perkins.
February 3, 1975 – June 28, 2018

Life Unfolding

SUE WHEELER
Arrived in 1974

I came west not to settle, but to earn enough money for an extended trip to Mexico. It seemed like my life was following a familiar path taken by many middle-class high school graduates in Ottawa. I had spent the summer and into the fall working as a clerk for the Department of National Defence. Transportation Operations seemed to involve bringing MPs' children home from Europe on free flights at summer's end. I remember watching the 1972 Canada-USSR hockey series on little televisions that we smuggled into work and the cheers that shook the building when we won!

Then it was off to Europe, clutching a five-hundred-dollar line of credit from my parents for emergencies and a battered copy of *Europe on 5 Dollars a Day*. Young people everywhere were on the move, criss-crossing Europe before going home or going farther east to Afghanistan, that romantic and exotic land. I so envied the lucky people who owned an afghan coat—the longer, shabbier and more embellished with embroidery, the better!

Afghanistan was not for me, though, and I headed to Crete, where people were flocking to live in or near the caves in Matala, a tiny town made famous by Joni Mitchell's song "Carey." Romantic and scary at the same time, Matala made a wonderful haven to pass the chilly winter. The caves in the mountainside had been home to lepers ostracized from mainland Europe, and now hippies were squatting in them and pulling out survey stakes planted by enterprising hotel chains. Every few weeks we'd board the local bus for the ride over the mountains to Heraklion, on to the ferry to Athens and then downtown to sell our blood in order to finance a few more weeks away. It was a carefree time with easy access to the pill and before AIDS, and the early days of hysteria and misunderstanding about that disease.

Back in Ottawa, it seemed like carefree travelling came to a screeching halt, and I was clearly expected to go to university. As luck would have it, though, a year at Trent University in Peterborough resulted in not only education but also romance and an invitation to embark on more travel and another adventure.

It was the fall of 1974. My introduction to BC and Vancouver Island was by car over the Rockies. For an Ontario-born girl, both the mountains and the ocean held allure. We planned that our friend Dick would drive us from Calgary to Long Beach for a week of camping and acclimatizing before we found work, ostensibly in Port Alberni, which would finance an extended trip to Mexico.

Reality quickly set in, though, as we found no work in the woods or in the many mills in Port Alberni. We finally got a contract along with another itinerant couple to build infrastructure for a new boat-in logging camp at Kennedy Lake, on the way to Tofino. There were trailer-type bunkhouses already there but no electricity or plumbing. We made ourselves comfy in these skeletons, cooking on camp stoves and entertaining ourselves during off-hours by learning to drive backhoes and other big pieces of equipment. None of us were carpenters or builders, but nonetheless we managed to build a huge generator house, complete with a double envelope of drywall on all sides for fire and noise suppression, and a water tower. Fallers arrived by boat each day and watched our progress, wide-eyed at our clothing (or lack thereof) and our unorthodox techniques.

Trying my hand at catching an elusive salmon with a knuckle-buster reel. Port McNeill, 1979.

After many months of us living in Port Alberni and Qualicum Beach, the trip to Mexico took shape. We acquired a lemon-coloured 1963 Econo-line van and camperized it to our satisfaction. I was thrilled with the "washing machine"—a ten-gallon bucket strapped to the roof rack! No elbow grease required. In the meantime, I had been captured by the ocean and the mountains. The excitement of picking oysters and digging clams and consuming the free bounty of the ocean made the Island seem like paradise. In winter, the lowest tides are at night, and I had groped in the muck in gumboots and headlamp, in the never-ending fog, drizzle or pelting rain. Little did I know that the lowest tides are in the daytime during the other seasons. I was amazed that these delicacies could be harvested in daylight!

One successful adventure and one failed romance later, I landed back in Ottawa, desperate to get back to the Island. I had heard of a program run by Malaspina College (now Vancouver Island University) in Nanaimo called Studies in Leisure Services. It sounded wonderful! A single telephone interview later and I was committed to two years of classes and a curriculum that included hikes, winter camping, canoe trips, bicycle trips and the promise of exploring many secrets of the outdoors on the Island.

It was a wild and carefree time. We bonded as a group and became fast friends; many of these friendships are still flourishing almost forty years

The height of fashion and independence: stretchy chocolate-brown velour short shorts and my '63 Rovin' Rambler.

later. Romances flared and fizzled, sometimes with great drama and other times with barely a murmur. I bought my first car with money from a student loan, a 1963 Rambler Classic station wagon with funky vacuum-assist windshield wipers. It wasn't just a car but a declaration of independence and a continuation of the freedom and joy of self-determination, and of embracing what unfolds. I was accepting invitations to parties down unknown dirt roads, dancing until closing time at the Moose Hall in Extension and quaking at the thought of a three-day wilderness "solo" at Horne Lake, a mandatory course requirement. We were dropped off around the lake, armed only with notebooks and sketch pads and a chunk of plastic to build a bivouac shelter. It was an initiation for me: no books or other distractions to deter me from being alone in nature.

As we gathered after our solos to share our experiences, I remember feeling so much compassion for Patti, who just couldn't do it, even when offered a camping spot just across the bay from our watchful instructors. On the other hand, Rudy, one of the very few of us born on the Island, told us that he'd bushwhacked all the way to the outskirts of Port Alberni, miles from the lake! So much for sitting quietly with himself. He was wearing a T-shirt that said Be Alert—The World Needs More Lerts, which seemed to sum up all of our various personalities.

My first glimpse of the Comox Glacier appeared en route to the drop-off point of a week-long September hike through Forbidden Plateau. Both the glacier, by name Queneesh, and the plateau were steeped in local First Nations history and mythology. We heard that the "red snow" (coloured by algae) found on the plateau was a reminder of women and children who had been slaughtered by hostile raiding parties. History aside, we were off on an adventure as the operator of the old chairlift on the ski hill loaded us aboard with our packsacks, dogs, contraband and ill-advised meal plans. In many spots, the ground seemed far away from our swaying chairs, especially with rocks below instead of the illusion of soft snow. We hooted and hollered as we soaked up the views of Georgia Strait and the small islands swimming in the foreground to a backdrop of the mainland mountains.

All along the trails, we enjoyed wild blueberries and kept our eyes peeled for the hungry black bears vying for the same berries. The majestic beauty of the plateau, with its quiet lakes and towering peaks, served as another hook, anchoring me to the Island and in particular to the Comox Valley.

Midway through the program, I took a practicum position at the old lodge on Forbidden Plateau, right at the base of the ski hill. A group of us would run the lodge and operate an outdoor centre that offered wilderness experiences year-round. It was a romantically ramshackle building, with the downstairs floors rolling like waves on the sea from years of frost heaves. Upstairs, a soaring fireplace dominated the dining room, where we served up medieval dinners complete with huge roasts, flatbread and a single knife for each guest to enjoy their feast. Costumes were wild and imaginative, and there was a stockade in the corner where guests would be manacled if they misbehaved!

Life at the lodge provided another new learning curve for me. The old generator had to be nursed along with regular oil changes, and evenings were spent enduring its ear-splitting drone in order to supply clients with the modern conveniences they were paying for. Learning that generator's complexities while quite competent men relaxed was another introduction to the "level playing field" of equality of the sexes in the seventies. Bah! Humbug!

Despite the lodge's quirks, our ever-changing guests' desire for wilderness experiences got us away from the noise of the generator. It was a time of intense learning as well: silviculture (a fancy name for learning about the forests and healthy practices for living in harmony with them), rock climbing and rappelling, orienteering, camping in all seasons and all weather, leadership and team building, and delivering memorable experiences for guests. The canoe rack would be hitched to Glenn's old Valiant with the push-button gearshift, and we would be off on a canoe trip to the Cruikshank River on Comox Lake. Newbies would come outfitted with freeze-dried food, while old hands would pull out steaks and bottles of wine, knowing full well we wouldn't have to carry anything, as the canoes would do the work! I was living the dream in the quiet and the camaraderie of like-minded folks.

Around this time the future of the lodge shifted and new faces found their way to Forbidden Plateau. Jamie and Gwyn Sproule became my lifelong friends as they took over stewardship of the old place. I was looking for permanence and solid roots in the valley I had come to love. I migrated to Courtenay, to steady work with the Courtenay Recreation Association. An old romance rekindled and we set our sights on buying a place to raise a family. I wonder if it was just coincidence or fate that I lived on Forbidden Plateau Road for the next decade?

With the purchase of a house, our priorities shifted and I learned to grow food and raise chickens and rabbits, and I felt great satisfaction when our pigs, named Sweet and Sour, became organic food for the family. When friends would gather, conversations went: "Have you got your peas in yet?" or "I canned three dozen jars of salmon" or "How did your salsa turn out?"

Relaxing on the dock with Monika Terfloth and daughter Tlell while waiting for the ferry from Beaver Cove to Sayward. Beaver Cove, 1979.

I learned to grow a bountiful garden and revel in the joy, laughter and love that come from shared feasts.

Today I indulge in the knowledge that my children, Jesse and Amber, love this valley and nurture strong connections to its landscape. Today I am thankful to have found John, my partner, in this valley. Today I am proud of the activists, the dreamers and the schemers who have helped the valley grow into a culturally rich and diverse community, where ideas are celebrated or protested with great gusto. Today I'm thankful for the family, friends and community that have nurtured and enriched my life these past forty years.

The Story I'm Compelled to Share

ANNE DAVIS
Arrived in 1974

Summer 1974. A hot and sunny day. I was nineteen years old, and I'd just set foot in the Comox Valley for the first time. My boyfriend and I had driven up from Victoria to participate in a craft fair—the very first Arts Alliance Renaissance Fair, held around the fountain beside the Sid Williams Theatre. I liked that fair and the people I met that day. They were young and creative and welcoming. One of them suggested we have a look at Cumberland, an old mining town nearby. We did and we fell in love with it, and two months later we were the proud owners and occupants of one of the old miners' houses on Camp Road.

So much of my life has flowed from that summer, in ways I could not possibly have imagined at the time. I knew, when we bought the house, that it had belonged to a retired miner and that he was now residing at the Bickle House, which at that time was a sort of old folks' home. On one of my first days in Cumberland, I walked up to the Bickle House to meet him, ask him some questions about the house and tell him how much we loved it.

When I met him, he sat me down and told me about Ginger Goodwin, the labour leader who was hunted down and shot in the hills behind Cumberland in 1918. I had never heard of Ginger Goodwin. I didn't grow up in a union household. Looking back, I think the seeds of my activism in the labour movement were planted on that day. As I listened to Jimmy talk about Ginger Goodwin with tears in his eyes, I understood that this was the story he felt compelled to pass on to a young person now living in his house. He was telling me that something important had happened in Cumberland and I needed to pay attention.

Home sweet home: life in a tool shed was cozy but challenging. Photo Anne Davis

Reflecting back on those years, I have so many sensory memories. I see candlelight, the light of oil lamps and the glint of silver on old shake-covered buildings. I hear music; it seemed as though there was always someone in the corner quietly playing an instrument. And the dances at the Arts Alliance: long-haired young men and young women in flowing dresses. Guitars, violins, mandolins. I feel warm sun on my shoulders as I work in the garden or sit in the sun with friends, gossiping and sharing ideas. We were so young and so sure of ourselves.

I learned a number of new skills: canning fruit and pickles, making bread, chopping and stacking firewood, keeping a fire going through the night in an old wood heater, growing my own vegetables, cooking on an oil stove, quilt making. At the same time, I was listening to the political commentary of activists around me who were working on issues of peace and social justice, and I was absorbing new ways of looking at the world.

Having been raised by a feminist mother, I was already well aware of many women's issues, but here in the Comox Valley, I found a community of women who were meeting together, sharing ideas and encouraging each other.

The relationship with my boyfriend didn't last. In 1976 we parted ways although, or because, I was pregnant. In the midst of turmoil, I distinctly remember the precise moment when I realized I was truly an adult, with adult problems and adult choices to make. I chose to have the baby and began preparing for life as a single parent. My friend Linda had recently had a baby, so we shared a house and planned to help each other. I was lucky to have a good job with the Youth Chance Society (later renamed Comox Valley Family Services) and access to maternity benefits, and I felt incredibly lucky to be part of a Comox Valley community that was supportive and encouraging. Friends and acquaintances provided everything I needed: crib, clothing, diapers, all of it.

The beach has always been my place of respite. Photo Bill Davis

Caitlin was born, and died, on June 15, 1977. My arms were empty and my heart was broken.

During my pregnancy with Caitlin, I had met the man I would marry and who would be the father of my four living children. With my share of the proceeds from the sale of the Cumberland house, I bought forested property in Merville, across the street from his equally forested property. We decided to build on his piece and spent a couple of years, whenever we had time, clearing an area for a house.

My daughter Emily was born in March of 1979. I cannot begin to describe the joy of holding her in my arms. That May, we moved into the tool shed on our property, using a large tent as a bedroom. Many of our friends were doing similar things—camping out on properties in Merville and Black Creek while building houses. Water came by way of a bucket dipped into the well, and we had the inevitable outhouse. Cloth diapers and

Baby Emily along for the ride. Merville, 1979. Photo Ella Davis

other laundry were hauled to the laundromat in town. We finally moved into our half-completed house on Halloween. Nights in the tent were cold by then!

Evan and Colin were born while we lived in Merville, and Alice arrived while we were living briefly in Comox before moving to Denman Island in 1989.

In the late eighties, I was asked if we could shelter, in our own home, women and children who were escaping violence. The new Comox Valley Transition Society was trying to secure funding for a transition house and had set up a network of safe homes in the meantime. We did that for three years, and then I was hired on at Lilli House when it finally opened. I've been with the Transition Society for twenty-five years now, in a number of positions, and am so proud of the women working here, of the women and children we serve, and of all we have done, and continue to do, in our community and beyond.

In the early nineties, I helped to organize the Transition Society into a union, the Health Sciences Association (HSA), and became active in the union, including several years as a regional director. I represented HSA on provincial and national union women's committees and got involved in the Labour Council, serving as a president and vice-president. The union has given me many opportunities for activism and political engagement.

By 2001 my marriage was long over and I had moved into a lovely old house in Courtenay. In 2005 I married Brian, a retired union educator. Children grew up and left home, returning with partners and grandchildren. I am growing older alongside friends I have known for my entire adult life. I'm still very active in my union and in the Labour Council, and I'm still involved every year in planning ceremonies and events to commemorate the life and death of Ginger Goodwin. I make a point of sharing that story with a younger generation. When I speak with young activists, that is the story I'm compelled to share.

Building an Unexpected Life

Nonie Caflisch
Arrived in 1974

Even from a very young age, when my father would ask what I wanted from life, my response was always "to be happy." When I reflect back, I can say I have been successful. I have lived a happy life, not without ups and downs, not without unexpected dramas and heartaches, but a happy life overall. Living in Merville for the past forty-three years has been a big part of creating that happiness in my life.

I grew up in Victoria in the fifties and sixties knowing I wanted to be a teacher. When I graduated from high school in 1970, I enrolled in the education program at the University of Victoria. My high school boyfriend, Rod, went off to the Vancouver School of Art. In the summer between first and second year, he decided not to go back to art school but to work and save money to travel Europe the following year. I decided I would take that year off and go too. He worked for a year and we banked his money. As I was in school, I didn't pay my parents room and board, but he paid his, so I worked evenings and weekends to cover that cost and our other expenses. In September of 1972, with three thousand dollars, we boarded a plane to London. We had an amazing year: hitchhiking, hostelling and for a time living in and camping from our car, making our way through Great Britain, Europe and Morocco. Having never travelled anywhere before and having led a sheltered, innocent life up until then, I found this experience life-changing. My eyes, heart and mind were opening to possibilities that I had never imagined, let alone dreamt of.

We returned to Victoria, back to what we knew. Rod worked and I returned to the university for my third year, which would complete my teaching certification. We married on International Women's Day in 1974. In those days, school districts sent people to the university to interview potential teachers. We had decided that we did not want to live in Victoria or Nanaimo, but we did want to stay on the Island. I would happily leave in the morning for a job interview, only to return in the evening to Rod being unwilling to move to Zeballos or whatever other place the interview was for. Finally we had the "Okay, where *would* you move to?" conversation. Rod had fond memories of summer vacations at Miracle Beach with his family, so we chose the Comox Valley. I interviewed with School District 71 and started teaching on June 1, 1974, at Royston Elementary.

Rod and me at our wedding on International Women's Day, March 8, 1974.

The first year, we lived in an oceanfront cottage in Union Bay that was right on the very noisy Island Highway, but with stunning views of Baynes Sound and Denman Island. One morning in the middle of winter, I woke to the most intense quiet I had ever experienced. It had snowed a few feet overnight and all traffic had stopped, as the highway was shut down. From our bedroom window, we watched two feet or so of snow undulate on the incoming tide, still a vivid picture in my mind forty years later.

A woman who was an itinerant teacher at Royston invited us to a New Year's party. She had been telling me that she and her husband had bought a five-acre share of a twenty-acre piece of land in Merville and were planning on building a house. At the party, we briefly met one of their land partners. A few months later, we answered an ad in the paper for a five-acre share of land with a small cabin. We went to look and naively decided it was for us. Family helped us finance the purchase. By then we knew it was the same piece of land my co-worker had bought into, but we didn't reconnect with the partner we had previously met or meet the other partner, who lived in Calgary. We were young and naive, and we happily moved into our three-hundred-square-foot cabin: no running water, a wood cookstove and an airtight heater, but with the luxury of electricity. We drove a 1949 Ford one-ton flat deck. We had a Siamese kitten named Cal. Merville became home.

Merville had a general store and a post office on the highway (don't blink, or you will miss it!), which was the hub of the community. At that time, the store was run by Jim and Rose, an older couple with hearts of gold, who easily extended credit and loved people. Jim, especially, always had time to chat at the deli counter. So many people from so many different places and backgrounds were looking to find a backwoods, back-to-the-land hideaway. I remember a conversation with a friend in which we discussed how different it was in a small community, where everyone seemed to know everyone else's business. A few minutes later, as I was given my mail—which included a postcard from Rod, who was away travelling—the clerk commented on what a good time Rod was having in Guatemala. I laughed: gotta love a small community! In turn, Lou and Tilly took over the store, followed by Terry and Robin. They all maintained the warm and inviting feeling of the Merville General Store.

Most of the people we met were busy tree planting, building, enjoying the river in the summer and sitting around the fire at potlucks in the winter. One of our first winters we were invited, along with our land partner Tony, to a New Year's dinner at one of the first places off Railway Avenue. It had snowed a few feet that day, but undeterred, we three drove down the hill in my less-than-reliable 1960 Morris Minor. We made it down Railway Avenue to where the side road was but had to leave the car there to walk the rest of the way. Our hosts were living in what was later to become their goat shed. I will never forget the look on their faces when we arrived, as they had been housebound for days due to the weather, and they had not much food and of course no telephone to call us and let us know not to come. It turned out to be a wonderful evening despite it all. I don't remember how we made it home, though we must have because there wasn't room in their cabin for us to stay over.

The hot summer days always ended with a swim in one of the swimming holes on the Tsolum River. As most of us were in various stages of building and not many of us had running water, the swim became our bathing time as well. Fortunately, in the cooler times of year, the community pool was available for a hot tub, sauna and shower. It would often turn into a social event as we "back to the landers" all got clean together while discussing our various and sundry projects.

Over the next few years, Rod went tree planting in the spring and fall and I taught during the school year, by then at the school in Black Creek. In the winter we collected building materials from buildings that were being demolished, and in the summer we started building our house in the woods. We built in the summer months with the money we had saved. We hand-built the stone footing and foundation, which took an entire season.

As we knew nothing about building with stone, except what we had read and Rod had studied over the winter, we started on the back side of the house and worked around to the front. By that time, Rod's artistic talents were in full swing and I had learned to backfill behind the foot-thick walls. It was nearing fall as we started on the tall wall on the front of the house, which features a round window trimmed with shaped sandstone. We had salvaged the sandstone blocks from the immigration building that was being demolished in Victoria and had only a finite number of them. They needed to be cut to fit around the round window in a sloping wall. We discovered, after losing a few in the process, that they were too cold early in the day to be cut reliably, but if left to warm in the sun for a few hours, they would co-operate nicely. Rod is a perfectionist, and the wall turned out beautifully and has been enjoyed immensely over the past forty years.

The next season we cut down long, straight fir trees approximately six inches in diameter, peeled, scraped and oiled them. These would seem very undersized for building, but they had grown in a gravel pit and were almost a hundred years old, with very tight growth rings, and very strong. They were then carved into mortise and tenon and fitted together to form the superstructure of what at that time looked like a giant Japanese birdcage in the forest. A beautiful sight!

The beginning of our dream in stone and wood.

Driving home in our '49 Ford.

My friend Gerri Minaker and I were recently talking about how normal it was in the seventies to swim naked at the river or to go to visit a neighbour and find them gardening naked. Things are not the same now, but it was quite normal back then in this neighbourhood. So on one of those hot summer days, as we were working on the poles for our house, I was wearing only sneakers and underpants. I was very hot and lamenting not having brought a hat. Being inventive, I decided I needed a hat more than I needed underwear, so I placed them on my head instead. As our driveway was a quarter-mile long and not very drivable even in summer, I wasn't expecting visitors. We were interrupted in our work by voices greeting us: three friends from high school had gone to a lot of effort to find us. There I stood, my underpants on my head, sneakers on my feet, to comments that they never dreamed in high school they would see so much of me! That goes down in my history as one of my most embarrassing moments!

The community of people is what has tied me to Merville. The work bees, helping each other with roofing, rock picking and land clearing, made the work so much easier. When a house on our land burned, the community rallied to support us, and I will forever be grateful. The dances at the Merville Hall, with gumboots lining the walls and babies sleeping under the tables, were such good times. By far the best tradition, started some forty years ago by Renee and her partner, was the winter solstice celebration. It started very small: a play enacted around a bonfire. If you came for the celebration, you were given a part, and they hosted a potluck at their house afterwards. Over the years, it grew. For some years in the eighties, it moved to our land. By then there was a script, with assigned roles and jobs. By far my favourite part was the way the paper-bag lanterns always marked the path through the forest to the pageant site. The last solstice celebration at our house was in the early nineties. By then, there were over one hundred people, too many for an indoor potluck, so some people had plates of food passed out the window. Now the Merville solstice pageant is back in the meadow where it started, with two hundred to three hundred people in attendance, along with a spectacular bonfire, little candle boats on the river and still the paper-bag lanterns to light the way. Numerous potlucks take place throughout the neighbourhood afterwards. The River Common community has recently donated the meadow as a park, and the solstice celebration will no doubt continue to evolve.

A lot has changed in my life along the way. Rod and I separated with our house only partially completed, but my next partner and now husband, Jonathan, is also a creative and accomplished builder that Rod had introduced me to when they both were working at Strathcona Park Lodge. So with Rod's blessing, Jonathan and I took over the completion. My friend Ray has asked a rhetorical question: "How many husbands do you think it will take for Nonie to finish her house?" My answer is still the same after thirty-eight years of being with Jonathan: "I am not sure; I am not finished yet." When we originally bought into the land, there were four shares. Now there are two: one of the original owners, Tony and his family, and us. We started out naively but lucked out with the land partnership we bought into.

Merville has been a wonderful community in which to live and raise a family. I have often thanked Rod for helping lead me here. His honest response when I suggested that Jonathan and I take over the building project was that in his mind he always saw me living here but not himself. He lives in Vancouver but visits often, and I am happily still a "Mervillite."

A Determined Feminist

DENISE NADEAU
Arrived in 1974

Beth and I were on our fifth fishing day trip out of Lund and we'd had no luck. In the fishing lingo of the time, we were skunked. The *Edna L* was an old wooden troller, built in the thirties, somewhat rickety, but it still had a commercial B licence for fishing salmon. The sun was getting high in the sky, so I said to Beth, "Let's take up our lines, as no salmon will be interested in biting midday." I moved over to the right hydraulic gurdy and pressed the gear. And it didn't work! I went to the other side and it was the same. Our lines were locked!

I called Beth, who was steering, to come and help me, but she didn't know what to do either. I had hired her as my crew through an ad in the *Georgia Straight*. She had crewed on a sailboat but didn't know a thing about fishboats. I had fished only one season with my former husband and basically was a city girl from Montreal on an adventure, with little knowledge or training. So here we were, about two miles out of Lund, unable to bring up our lines. We couldn't pilot the boat in, as the lines, thirty metres down and with heavy iron cannonballs at the tips, would just drag on the bottom once we got closer. All I could think of was how embarrassing it was: all the guys on their fishboats would laugh at us! After my panic had subsided, we decided to haul up the lines by hand, a job that took us hours and left a deck full of twisted cable. Our hands and hearts were raw as our boat limped into the harbour at dusk.

My stint as a woman fisher was short, in fact only six weeks in the summer of 1975. But I loved being the captain and fishing with another woman in what was and still is a male-dominated world. In August I returned the boat to Comox, where my former husband waited his turn to take it out.

Two words that defined my experience of the seventies were feminism and determination. In fact, feminism shaped my determination, fuelling me sometimes with sheer willpower, to do things I would have never considered before.

I arrived in Courtenay in 1974 with my then husband and the *Edna L.* We chose Comox, actually the Courtenay Slough, as a place to dock our boat. We rented a small house on Scott Road, just off Dyke Road. We didn't want to live in Nanaimo where his parents lived. We both hoped to find winter work in this smaller community, which seemed so beautiful with its glacier, the mountains and the sea. However, the marriage was short-lived. Another boat incident was symbolic of our relationship challenges. We were crossing Georgia Strait, heading for Vancouver, when a gale suddenly arose. I was terrified as the swells grew larger and larger, the wind howling, and I begged him to turn back as he steered us through giant waves. He turned to me and yelled, "There can only be one captain on a boat and that's me!"

That was the end of the relationship for a serious feminist like me. In 1970 in Montreal, I had been part of a women's group where we all shared how oppressed we were by both men and patriarchal structures in our lives. In the following three years, I lived in Britain while I attended graduate school, and I became involved in socialist feminism and Wages for Housework. Both were concerned about women's poverty and the invisibility of women's labour, as well as women's reproductive rights. When I arrived in the Comox Valley, I found a back-to-the-land feminism, with aspects of goddess religion thrown into the mix. I added both to my world view, resolute in my commitment to be in control of my body and my life. Whether it was gutting a salmon, building my own cabin or throwing a feminist tarot deck, I was determined to challenge the patriarchy at all levels.

The Comox Valley was a hotbed of strong women. We came from different backgrounds and sexual orientations, but most of us were white. We were determined to take control of our lives. The idea of having a Women's Festival arose, a place where we could practise new skills and share what we had learned on our various journeys. I can't remember exactly how it happened, but I ended up on the planning committee for the first Women's Festival. Susan Holvenstot offered Port H'kusam, where she had a share in the land, and we accepted because it was isolated and promised to be a real adventure. We could take off our clothes and have no men interfering in our workshops and celebrations. To get to H'kusam in the Sayward Valley, one had to hike several kilometres on a dirt road full of potholes, over a small mountain. Janet, a bus driver, offered to drive a four-by-four van she had borrowed for those who couldn't do the hike. I helped her load and unload the camping gear and packs. I gave a workshop; I have no memory of the

Where should we dig another outhouse? Judy and I dealt with more women arriving than expected at the Women's Festival in 1977.

subject now. I remember Susan Holvenstot did one on how to use a chainsaw. And several lesbians came from Vancouver and Errington to offer a workshop, which I attended, as I was deeply curious.

That year at H'kusam I was pregnant. I was living with my son's father and working on building a cabin on a piece of land in Black Creek that I had bought into with him and Diana. Diana was a lesbian whom I had met and shared a house with for a while in Comox after I had split up with my husband. She was building a circular cabin and inspired me to build my own, as I was anxious to have my own space. My new partner helped me a lot with the cabin, though at that time I didn't really acknowledge how much he helped with the design and some of the construction. Both Diana and I had entered the world of women's do-it-yourself carpentry, and were confident we could do anything.

I was determined to have a home birth, which at that point was not supported by the medical establishment; midwifery was illegal in British Columbia. Stories of home birthing by Ina May Gaskin and the Farm Midwifery Center were coming to us from the United States, as well as the book *Our Bodies, Ourselves*, which was our bible for self-care and rejection of male control of women's health. We even had a small women's health group for a while, a few of us gathering with plastic speculums and mirrors to do our own pelvic exams. I didn't want my birth experience stolen from me by the doctors at St. Joseph's Hospital. Luckily, I found Gloria Simpson from Cumberland, who agreed to be my midwife. My baby was due in January. Suspecting it would snow, I arranged with a friend to have the birth at her house in Comox, practically across the street from the hospital. Sure enough it did snow, and I successfully delivered my baby at "home," what may have been one of the first home births in the valley in a long time, at least amongst the recent white settlers.

If the slogan "The personal is political" was an overriding theme of this decade, my experience in Britain had made me much more aware of the larger structural issues facing women: in particular, spousal abuse and its relationship with women's poverty and lack of economic options. In the fall of 1978, I saw an advertisement for a job posted by Status of Women Canada, a job that addressed the issue of spousal abuse. The seventies were a time of federal Liberal largesse, with funding for programs like Katimavik and women's programs. I applied and got the job as coordinator of the Women's Services Train-

My son, Kael, and me at the Women's Festival in 1976, with my friend Joy in the background.

ing Program for Vancouver Island. This national project involved seven rural regions in Canada and focussed on the needs of women abused by their spouses in single-industry resource communities.

With an ad hoc hiring committee, I was able to employ six women in five communities on Vancouver Island: Port Alberni, Campbell River, Port McNeill, Port Hardy and the Comox Valley. I was becoming slowly aware of the issue of the ongoing discrimination and violence against Indigenous women, but I managed to hire only one First Nations woman, a Nuu-chah-nulth from Port Alberni. Like most government programs, the Women's Services Training Program, with one person per town to do counselling and advocacy over a one-year period, was totally unrealistic in terms of dealing with the causes and consequences of domestic abuse in resource-based communities. At that time, in all of these communities, there were no shelters or transition houses and only a few "safe homes." In the Comox Valley, because there were the three towns—Comox, Cumberland and Courtenay—to cover, not to mention Denman and Hornby Islands, we hired two women, both now deceased: Lee, a deeply compassionate and thoughtful presence who helped many women with one-on-one counselling, and Jean, advocate extraordinaire.

After eight months of uncovering the extent of the problem, and seeing that one counsellor/advocate per town was not even an effective band-aid, Jean insisted we go for more money and a bigger vision. In 1979, with her drive and brilliance and my determination, we wrote a hundred-page application for three years of funding from Health Canada as a "demonstration grant." We got it and formed the Women's Self Help Network, which developed a training program for self-help groups, provided jobs for many women in four Island communities and produced training manuals, which later sold across the country for more than a decade. Many of the women who were part of the core collective that developed this project had met at the Women's Festivals.

By the end of the seventies, I was out as a lesbian, in a context where lesbianism was often seen as a political act. Luckily, I had a son, so I wasn't into lesbian separatism, a movement that had some support in our rural area. The fact that so many out lesbians could live unharmed in the Comox Valley indicates the extent to which a counterculture had permeated this community.

My relationship with the Comox Valley has been long but bittersweet. In the early eighties, my son's father and I were in a custody case over my son, where my lesbianism became an issue. Though we eventually turned to mediation, my joint custody status was premised on my son continuing to be with his dad's new family. As someone who entered the field of ministry and religious studies in the mid-eighties, my job options were outside the Comox Valley. Accordingly, I had a back-and-forth relationship with the valley, as did my son. When he decided he wanted to be in the valley for all of high school, I returned full-time and bought a house in Royston. I didn't want to be back, but my relationship with my son was more important. It turned out those years in the early nineties were extremely valuable for me. I got to know women and men in the progressive labour movement in the Comox Valley, and I became involved in issues of women's labour rights.

I kept the house after my son graduated, but I returned to the city, alternating between Vancouver and Montreal for work. I basically have had a commuting relationship with the valley for over three decades. I moved back full-time in 2008, the negative feelings from the past over, very happy to be in a place where I knew and loved the land, the waterways, the mountains and the glacier. I still continued to work part-time in Montreal and Vancouver. As I write this in 2018, I have recently moved to a condo in Victoria, where my son and his family live.

What has stayed with me from the seventies is my feminism, though it's a lot more nuanced. I am now aware of my own class and race privilege that allowed me to do many of the things that I thought were achieved because of my determination. I certainly had a lot of willpower, as well as the illusion that I was in control of my life, one that was quickly shattered as I grew older. My feminism continues to be political in that I lobby against structures that limit women and their families, including the Indian Act and ongoing colonial structures that target Indigenous women, refugees and people of colour. I no longer see salmon as prey for money; now, salmon are relatives whose bodily integrity is greatly threatened by open-net fishing farms, pollution and overfishing. I have traded in goddess religions for the feminine face of god and interfaith solidarity. I am now aware I am an un-invited visitor in the territory of the K'omoks peoples.

What I hold dear from those years of the seventies in the Comox Valley is the fervour and commitment of the women with whom I walked along-side, our refusal to compromise our bodies and our selves, and the holding of a vision that was larger than each of us. From those years I learned the importance of continuing to fight not only for all women's bodily and spiri-tual integrity, but also for that of all living beings. I am grateful that this has never left me.

Merville, My Home

OLIVE SCOTT
Arrived in 1975

I first set foot on Vancouver Island in 1959, when I travelled with my then boyfriend (now husband), David, to meet his parents, who lived in Victoria. The die was cast; the Island kept drawing me back! I taught in Port Alberni in 1960, made more visits to Victoria, camped at Long Beach and in 1970 travelled through the Comox Valley en route to Gold River and camped on the south shore of Nootka Island. That trip confirmed for me that Vancouver Island was the place to live. At that time my husband and I lived in a rented house in Vancouver and I was a teacher in West Vancouver.

We often talked with friends about moving out of the city to raise our families. Not long after the camping trip, we met a couple who lived in a geodesic dome in Merville. They invited us to stay weekends with them and explore the Comox Valley, an offer that we happily accepted. We spent several happy weekends in Merville, meeting interesting, friendly people and looking at property. Though we explored much of the Comox Valley, Merville continued to attract our interest.

The seventies were an exciting time to be a teacher in BC. The population was growing and jobs were plentiful. The educational leadership in the province was progressive and open to innovative ideas. What more could early-career teachers anxious to move out of Vancouver ask for than to be hired to work in School District 71 in 1975?

Once we had jobs, we decided to buy some land and build a house. Never ones to do things by halves, we found recently logged acreage in Merville. It was a sunny day in May when we visited the property, and after the real estate agent left, we found a grassy spot and napped in the sunshine. When we awoke we were convinced that this was the land to buy. It was within our financial reach, and the manager at the credit union helped, to our amazement, by granting us a 100 percent mortgage on the undeveloped land.

Another lively discussion in the Georges P. Vanier Secondary School staff room.

Having spent my childhood and teens in small communities, I looked forward to moving to Merville. We purchased two used canvas tents to live in while we built. Our children, Jen, aged six, and Chris, almost three, played in the sun and helped when they could. We brought with us from Vancouver a dozen chicks that were a going-away present to my husband from his students. We managed to keep them alive and they grew into great egg layers. A henhouse was one of the first things we built.

I was tasked with wiring the house, and while buying the *Canadian Electrical Code Handbook* and materials at Central Builders Supply store, I met and became a regular customer of Bob, who was most generous with his advice and encouragement. To my delight, the wiring passed inspection.

As we had only two months to close in our dwelling, the pace was hectic. But with a hired youth and the labour of generous friends, we moved into an unfinished shell, with no power or running water and holes covered with plastic sheeting for windows, just before the rains began in late August. In the kitchen were makeshift shelves, a wood-burning cookstove, Coleman lamps and a cooler of ice. We carried water from Courtenay in five-gallon containers. The arrival of the fall rains made it clear why Merville was called "gumboot country," as the bottom of our driveway immediately became a mudhole and we were unable to drive our vehicles close to the house! I also learned of the generosity of Merville residents when a neighbour arrived with a load of gravel to fill the mudhole. When my mother came for a visit in the fall, she clearly thought I had lost my mind when she saw that I had opted for a wood cookstove and outhouse.

September arrived and we began our teaching jobs. I was a school counsellor and taught foods, then child care, then psychology at Georges P. Vanier Secondary School, grades 11 and 12 at that time. It was a dream job, almost like teaching at a junior college. The students were quite mature, and there were a number of recently hired young teachers who were full of energy and exciting ideas about teaching. One of the teachers, Linda Rajotte, had been a student teacher I had met in West Vancouver. We renewed our acquaintance at Vanier and have remained close friends. I was proud to work with such a progressive staff and administration. The school building was only a few years old, built in a time when there was federal money available for facilities for occupational training. As a result there were well-equipped specialty areas, including a plastics shop, large art rooms, a music room large enough to accommodate a full band or a large chorus, a cafeteria where students spent one day in four learning cooking skills and a staff dining room. Many great discussions took place over lunch prepared by the students. Soon after I settled into my office as the new counsellor in the valley, one of the public health nurses came knocking on my door. The Comox Valley Health Unit was assisting in the set-up of a Planned Parenthood clinic, and she asked if I would like to volunteer. Of course I agreed and spent Tuesday evenings in the basement of the health unit, assisting in the clinic. The irony is that I became pregnant that winter, unplanned, with our third child, Alex.

We enrolled Jennifer at Tsolum Elementary School, and we dropped Chris each day at Merry Andrew Day Care. I worked and showered at Vanier, and the kids were bathed at friends' homes. An unexpected advantage of an outhouse is that nature is close by. One evening my young son and I saw an amazing meteor on our way to the biffy. During the fall, insulation was placed and the windows were installed, and by Christmas 1975 the power was connected and we had lights for our tree. A wood heater kept the house cozy, but it was April before our well was drilled and we had running water and an indoor toilet. With the optimism and energy of youth, our hippie shack gradually evolved into a comfortable finished house with a landscaped yard.

During the second summer, we decided that our family needed a dog. After seeing an ad in the Merville General Store, we purchased a beautiful adult Great Dane. He was friendly and seemed to settle in, but one day he

Taking a break from building the sunroom, with the garden and chicken house in the background.

ran away and was found near the store. The clerk there remembered that we had bought the dog and contacted us to repatriate him. He seemed to settle in again until one afternoon, as we were sitting on the deck, a truck drove up, and a man got out and called the dog, which immediately ran to him. The man told us that he had been away for a while, and his ex-girlfriend had become tired of looking after the dog and put him up for sale. He had learned from friends in Merville where his dog was living. We accepted his refund of our money and he drove away with a happy dog. The children missed him but understood that "our" dog was glad to find his master. He was the first of many dogs, a constant in our life.

One afternoon in our third summer, a couple who had owned our property in 1922 arrived at our house and showed us where their dwelling had been. Later, we found pieces of a wood-burning cookstove in that area. I later learned that Merville had been settled by World War One veterans, and I couldn't help but wonder if the man had been one of them.

When I reflect on moving to Merville, I immediately think of the joy of raising a family in a rural setting adjacent to a town, now a city, with great schools and all the services a family needs. From the beginning, the children always had ways of contributing to the family: hammering nails, carrying firewood, feeding the chickens, gathering eggs and feeding the pony. They all three have grown to be healthy, responsible people who love nature and the outdoors. The wilds of Merville provided lots of adventures for our family: raccoons killing our chickens, a wolf stalking our pony and calf, sightings of cougars, bears, eagles and turkey vultures. The nights were starry and free of light pollution; the days were sunny and warm, or snowy, or rainy and cold. With not a neighbour in sight, it was like living in our own wilderness park.

However, neighbours there were, friendly and generous with information and ideas that at times saved us from making costly mistakes. But for a word from a neighbour, we might have placed our house in a boggy area! It was an advantage to already know people when we moved to Merville, as we were invited to potlucks and house parties, invitations that we reciprocated, and life was lively and fun. For me the bonus of living in the Comox Valley is the coterie of amazing colleagues that I taught with, the interesting people that I have met and the lifelong friends that I have made.

Thin Tin

PHYLLIS VICTORY
Arrived in 1975

And what *does* practising the tai chi Standing Tree Exercise in the middle of the bridge that crossed the Tsolum River, on the Hermitage, in Merville, have to do with any of it? Well, I suspect, everything.

Knees slightly bent. Back straight. Feet parallel. Arms held chest high, forming an open circle in front of my body. Searching for centre, that place where timelessness becomes a reality. I stood there, with my teacher, as thousands of spawning, battered salmon swam toward us up the river. An intense, immense wave of brilliant red and green fish slipped under the bridge and us. We stood there, as if two ancient trees, for what seemed like years. A silent witnessing for these salmon and to the exquisite poetry of it all.

In the spring of the next year, I went in search of a small cabin. Fitzgerald Road. Seventy dollars a month. Yes. My unemployment insurance cheque could cover that nicely and leave some extra to feed us. I said yes to the landlord and prepared to move in. On moving day, as I was about to drive over the bridge that ran across the creek, there, sitting on a branch at eye level, was a bald eagle. My precious, romantic, adventurous little self whispered, "I'm sure this is a sign!" My kids (who, I feel compelled to add here, actually turned out to be extremely fine human beings, and more importantly, still *love* me) and I sat in our car and stared at the eagle for a few minutes until slowly I began to feel this psychic, restless pressure filling the car as they wordlessly shouted, *Let's get on with this, already, Mom.* We crossed over the bridge.

Rounding the corner about a quarter of a mile from the bridge, we saw it: home! A small cabin about twenty feet from the road, near an open field. It looked romantic, picturesque and certainly humble, for it had no running water and no electricity, but I had spotted a power pole next to the house when I first went to look at it, and the owners had assured me that power was close at hand. Perfect! Electricity for our sound systems! I loved music; it was the panacea that boosted my morale and structured the minutes and moods of my day. I could float along on the deep, soulful notes of the *Pavane for a Dead Princess*, or ponder the depths of meaning with Paul Horn's *Inside the Taj Mahal*. I could close my eyes and go for an exquisite ride inside the lyrics of songs by Ann Mortifee (who, at a concert in Vancouver, gifted me with the beautiful image of "Kiss the Joy As It Flies," her adaptation of a poem by Blake). Or I could climb the "Stairway to Heaven" with Led Zeppelin. In my more uplifted moments, I could chant "Om Sri Ram Jai Ram Jai Jai Ram" with Swami Ramdas of Anandashram in Kerala. Oh yes, life was about to get really good. I had a dream. I was going to write a grant application to start a bagel factory with a friend in Victoria. It was the seventies, and bagels had not yet found their way to Victoria. I had already paid a hundred dollars to the Humble Bagel Factory in Eugene, Oregon, for their famous bagel recipe, and now I needed a cheap place to live and some quiet time in the country to write this grant application and to explore country life with my kids for about six months. Then we would be ready for the next adventure. Yes.

It seemed roomy for a three-hundred-square-foot cabin, but then, the furniture had not arrived. There was a wood stove, a five-foot built-in bed, a tiny kitchen and a small bedroom. Big enough, if I slept in the living room, for a single mother, a ten-year-old, a seventeen-year-old and two cats.

The first two weeks went by very quickly, and the repercussions of this romantic notion began to sink in. *What was I thinking?* The power pole *was* there next to the house, but as I discovered in a lengthy phone call to BC Hydro, "a temporary pole can only be used ONCE to connect up electricity," and that "once" had already been used up, certainly not by me and certainly not to power this small cabin. No amount of pleading could get them to even consider uttering the word "twice." So no music for me to float myself into my days; no music for a seventeen-year-old to be grooving on; no music at all! Which also meant: no refrigerator, no vacuum cleaner, no blender, no circulating oil heater and no LIGHTS! But what about my dream, my dream of sitting down at my round oak table (that now took up the whole kitchen) and writing my grant proposal? Surely I could trust that? That divine inspiration, that divine guidance? *Just trust*, a sliver-sized thought whispered into my ear, so quietly that I had to strain to hear it. *Surrender.* Knees slightly bent. Back straight. Feet parallel. Arms held chest high, forming an open circle in front of my body. Searching for centre. Damn!

At some point within the next month, my daughter decided it was time to live in a grown-up world that had electricity, transportation and easy access to her friends, so she moved in with her boyfriend in town. I didn't blame her; this lesson wasn't hers, and Merville was a long way from town. It was, however, one of the special places in the world where one could safely take a quantum leap into the unknown and eventually learn how to shape-shift. Somehow I knew that that was right where we were headed.

Then there was the airtight. Ah, the airtight. It was about three feet high and about two feet wide. It was made of a thin metal, very thin. Probably tin. Thin tin. I like that, thin tin. Okay, it was oval, this thin tin (I do love the way that sounds, the way the words play in my mouth), and the stove (I resisted saying it that time) was about six inches from the wooden wall of the corner of the living room and four inches from the wooden floor. Thin tin.

So now I had a stove and a woodshed but no firewood and no axe, but I did have enough money to buy Presto Logs and I did know where I could buy them. Safeway! I drove the twenty-five miles into Courtenay and bought the coveted Presto Logs and some matches. Back at my small cabin, my son and I unloaded the two boxes of Presto Logs from my VW Bug and carried them into the house. I popped one into the airtight stove, lit it and *voila*! Instant heat to take the chill off of the night air. Success! I'm a country woman now!

The only problem now was that the airtight was three feet high and Presto Logs are only five inches high. Since the log was burning in the bottom of the airtight, the heat was not getting to the top of the stove. I found that even if I used two Presto Logs, stacking them on top of each other (they were flat after all), the bottom of the stove would get so hot that it would glow red, right next to the wood on the wall, but there still wasn't enough heat to even warm a pot or a kettle. Thin tin, indeed.

We adjusted. We made frequent trips to the Merville General Store to do our laundry and buy fresh food that didn't need a lot of refrigeration, and the summer rolled slowly by with only the occasional need for a fire. The woman who was in the bagel caper with me backed out, and my enthusiasm for starting a bagel factory slowly shrivelled. My son learned to pull buckets of water, along with the occasional snake and toad, from the well in the front yard, and we bathed in the Tsolum River behind our house.

Life got simpler and simpler. My son made friends with the boys in the neighbourhood. He loved riding his bike through the woods, past the Old Mill, to visit his friend at the Hermitage. He had become a country boy *and* a city boy and was now at ease in both worlds. Perfect! *I* began to be aware of the patterns in space that my body was making by driving to the Merville Store and to Courtenay and by walking to the river. The geometry of my life, I guess you could call it. The lines were simple lines but I began to experience them as this lovely pattern of simplicity, and I could "see" them as beams of light suspended in space. I ate foods according to their colours and found myself drawn to eating oranges and yogurt. I spent days chanting on the one flat rock in the middle of the river as the silky water flowed all around me. Life was good.

One late afternoon there was a knock at the door. The neighbour from across the road had come for a visit. He introduced himself and sat down in the antique rocker next to the airtight. I explained that I would have offered him tea, but I never could get the water to boil. So he chatted on and on in the way that country people do, while they are waiting to get to the point of telling you why they have come. It takes so long...and then the words come out of their mouths, as if the letters have been hanging out in the cracks between their teeth, waiting for the right moment to form themselves into words. Finally the "real" words found the divine command that they had been waiting for and they formed themselves into words and were spoken. "Phyllis" —he called me by my name now—"I've been noticing that you've been buying PRESTO LOGS!" The words had erupted out of his mouth and flew around my small cabin now, bouncing off of my quiet wooden walls, slipping into their own dusty cracks. I guiltily muttered, "Yes?" I was sure that I had now been expelled from the "country woman" status. Yikes, someone had been watching me! "Well, did you know," he continued on, letting more words escape into the heavy air, "that there is a shake mill down the road, on Merville Road?" I thought to myself, *Oh no! I'm not ready!* I wasn't ready to figure out how to do all of that. I had been comfortably sitting in the river, chanting to God during the days and in the evenings burning my beloved Presto Logs. "Well, thank you, I didn't know that," I said, attempting to look very interested and eager to receive this bit of country wisdom. Having delivered his helpful message, he must have felt complete, because all of his words except "goodbye" had been used up. Thin tin.

Over the next month there *were* changes, but I wasn't ready to change everything, having found a groove that was so simple and easy. So I still went to Safeway to buy my beloved Presto Logs, but now, instead of guiltlessly bringing them into the house during the light of day, they waited, hidden in the back of my VW until the dark of night. Then I crept quietly out to bring them in without even a flashlight to guide my way, not giving even one tiny clue that they were still a part of my life.

The neighbour returned one more time, in late summer, to deliver another message. More words. More waiting. This time the procedure was the same; he still waited until the letters magically made themselves into words, but this time it was different. As he sat there in the same rocking chair, by the same airtight, Thumper, my very large orange-and-white cat, jumped into his lap. The neighbour sat there, petting Thumper as if they were old, best friends. When the "real" words showed themselves, it was Thumper that he had come to talk about. Seems that Thumper had been jumping into the old car that he had stored on his property and peeing in it. And because it was summer and hot, it was beginning to smell really bad. And would I please keep Thumper at home? (I laughed uproariously to myself, and sternly disciplined my eyes.) His words used up once again, he gently put the guilty cat down on the floor and left. Keep Thumper at home? Ha ha ha. We had no fence, no cat door to lock, no gate and both cats had learned how to pull on the cord to open the back door to let themselves in and out. Keep Thumper at home? Well, *that* wasn't going to happen. However, I *did* have a heart-to-heart talk with Thumper and asked him very nicely, but firmly, to please not pee in the neighbour's car, because he

Chilly spring bathers rushing from the Tsolum River to the infamous cabin, which was rumoured to have once been a rabbit hutch! The neighbour's house is in the background. Photo Phyllis Victory

really didn't like it. I hoped that it had helped and that there were no more incidents, but since no more words were coming from the neighbour, I'm not sure if Thumper ever complied.

It took another month and the coming of fall before I was truly ready. I found the shake mill, bought an axe and ordered a cord of wood to store in the woodshed. I brought in boxes of shakes during the light of day so that the neighbour could see that his helpful hint had been duly received. I learned how to make beautiful and safe fires, invited friends for tea and actually *boiled* the water. I even discovered how to cook with a jaffle iron by thrusting the iron down into the flames, and I became famous for making a killer toasted egg-and-cheese pocket-bread sandwich. We had sponge baths in the house and generally made it all work. That cabin and piece of land had become a polished mirror, which would show me every tiny, single blemish on my perfectly imagined self. A few years later, when my son and I finally left, it was only because he had grown too large for his five-foot bed.

My final measure of success came when I was out riding in my car with one of my dearest and closest friends. We drove past my cabin. He "got" the magic of that small cabin, the copper hanging pot with lobelias on the porch, the small rainbow windsock and the mandala garden. He turned to me and said, "Wow! I wonder who lives *there?*"

I do.

Embracing Change

LINDA RAJOTTE
Arrived in 1976

I am a person who has always lived in the moment. Therefore, trying to remember details of my time in the seventies in the Comox Valley presents some problems. I remember close friendships, love, my growing family, a sense of wonder at the beauty of the valley and a sense of home, but I don't live in the past.

I treasure my time in the Comox Valley not only for what it was but also for what I have become because of this very special period, when so many things were changing for women in the world. The sixties and seventies were exhilarating times to grow up, to develop strength as an independent woman, to experience natural childbirth and to know the wonder of those small, trusting hands that fit so easily into mine. As a generation, we were indeed blessed to come of age in this time and in such a vibrant, welcoming haven as the Comox Valley.

I came to the valley in 1976, and I felt like I was coming home after a very long journey. I had moved around for many years; it was time to settle down. The fact that I lived in the valley for the next twenty-six years of my life simply astounds me. My family moved from place to place, because my father worked for the telephone company; with each promotion, we were transferred to a new town. My mother would tell my brother and me about the exciting new place we would be living in the following year. From my mother, I learned how to embrace change as an adventure, how to fully experience each day and how to adapt to a new environment.

I was an academic who enjoyed learning. At the University of British Columbia, I studied mathematics and was often the only female in my upper-level classes, but it didn't bother me, because I had such love for this beautiful subject. It never occurred to me that this field of study was gender specific. I also took art courses, and I understood that mathematics was an art as well. I later brought that feeling into my teaching and wanted my students to experience the wonder, the creativity and the passion that I felt for mathematics.

My first teaching job was in 1973 in the Queen Charlotte Islands (now Haida Gwaii). I arrived there with my husband, John, a kind and gentle man who still lives there. I was twenty-three years old, not that much older than my senior secondary students.

In 1975 I left the Charlottes with Roger, who was a naturally talented history teacher. It was the seventies, after all, and relationships were shifting. In our interview for our teaching jobs in Courtenay, Roger and I told our prospective employer that we were engaged. In the seventies, teachers were supposed to be respectable. When I came to Georges P. Vanier Secondary School, the principal assumed I was married by then. I told him that we weren't married yet but would be soon (this happened the following summer), which he graciously accepted. My father, who was very conventional, asked Roger when we were going to "legitimize our relationship," and my future husband said truthfully that we would do so once I was divorced. The times they were a-changin'!

When I arrived in the valley, the glacier was an amazing presence towering over Fifth Street. It made me feel safe, and I loved the wonder and the beauty of it. The air was clean, and the town was still small enough; on the main street, I knew every second person. Forbidden Plateau was the place to ski; Mount Washington Resort was not yet a reality. The Renaissance Fair was in full swing, and I embraced the laughter, the freedom and the music. Courtenay had a sense of community, of belonging, and a feeling that things were changing. It was an exciting time in the Comox Valley.

Perhaps the most important reason I moved to the valley was that my brother had died in 1973 and I wanted to be close to my parents, who lived in Campbell River. Dear friends had encouraged us to consider moving to the valley. Even though they later moved back to Australia, I developed other friendships that have lasted a lifetime. I think of them as "friends of the heart" who became our family, so much so that our children called them Auntie Rosemary, Uncle Ric, Auntie Debbie and Uncle Frank.

We had so much energy in the seventies and early eighties. Rosemary Vernon and I were always creating something for our children: smocked outfits, bear backpacks, Christmas wrapping paper of stars and hearts, or painted handprints by our children. To my delight, another friend moved to the valley, someone I had known since I was eight years old. Lynda Glover and I reunited in this magical place, and we made art together, had children

In 1979, Roger and I were young, ready for anything and looking into our bright future. How precious to remember this time.

together and are still best friends. We painted fish T-shirts, and we made indigo batiks, watercolour quilts, hand-painted silk scarves and so much more. Lynda is a true artist, and I embraced whatever new project we took on. Friendship, love and family surrounded me.

In our first year in the valley, we rented a little house on Headquarters Road, surrounded by fields. I woke up to the mist hanging over the land, experiencing the beauty and simplicity of my new home. Roger brought home a kitten that took care of the mice. We held an open house and forgot to send out many invitations (again, it was the seventies). So, when David and Olive Scott arrived with their two young children, we spent the entire afternoon drinking sangria, eating and beginning a long-lasting friendship. The Scotts held many parties in their house over the years. One memorable one was to celebrate David's fortieth birthday (we thought that was old at the time). David was making his own wine, and I painted a T-shirt for him with my hand-drawn original "Sir Scott Estate" crest on the front.

In 1980 our daughter, Chantelle, was born in St. Joseph's Hospital in Comox. Every time I drive by that hospital, I think of the nurse saying "Happy Mother's Day" as she presented me with my beautiful daughter all wrapped up tightly in her receiving blanket. I knew absolute love when looking at my baby girl, the overwhelming, unconditional, ferocious love of a mother.

We moved, buying our first home on Millard Road with the Courtenay River Estuary as our front yard. The trumpeter swans were just one part of the beauty and diversity of this magical place where the river meets the sea.

Our son, Daniel, was born in 1984 at the hospital in Comox. I never had an ultrasound with either of my children. This may seem strange today, but it was very common then. Two mornings before Daniel was born, we discovered that he was breech. My doctor's comment to me was that "the birth canal has been tested" and I was not to worry! Of course I was concerned, since most women had a Caesarean section for breech births. I arranged for a specialist, and fortuitously, my water broke the day I was to see him. He, my doctor, Roger and a nurse were with me for Daniel's birth. It wasn't easy but in a few hours, Daniel came into the world naturally, bringing his gentle nature and joy into our lives.

With two children, we were outgrowing our home by the estuary, so we bought our second house on Glen Urquhart Drive. It had inspirational views of the Comox Glacier, Mount Washington, Farquharson Farms and the distant ocean. Light flooded into our living space every day and reflected the breathtaking nature of the valley. We lived in this stunning house for the rest of my time in Courtenay.

Our children grew up in a much different way than I did. They lived in one place. They graduated with friends they had known since kindergarten, and they had a sense of a comforting hometown. Both Chantelle and Daniel have grown into confident, caring young adults who enjoy their professions. They understand that the valley gave them a wonderful start in life. Motherhood was the best thing that could have happened to me. I am forever grateful to my children and, now, my grandchildren.

In 1985 another tragedy struck my family: my father died in a fishing accident near Ucluelet on the west coast of Vancouver Island, when a killer wave overturned his boat. Fire had killed my brother, and water killed my father. I became overly fearful for my children's safety, and perhaps more protective than necessary. I held them very tightly to me. I also realized the importance of being close to my mother, since there were only two of us left from our original family of four. I treasure a photo of my mom, dad, Chantelle and Daniel taken just before Dad went on the fishing trip. Again, I was reminded that we couldn't predict what might happen in life, so we must live in the moment!

In teaching, I moved into a profession dominated by men. I was the only female mathematics teacher in my first few years at Vanier. In so many ways, my students taught me how to be a teacher. Mathematics had always come easily to me, and I remember a time very early on in my career in Courtenay when I was teaching a rather difficult topic to a group of advanced students in an honours class. I had worked hard on my lesson plan and thought I had done a good job until one of my best students approached me at the end of the week and quietly said that neither he nor any of the other students had understood a word I had said in the last three lessons! I realized then that teaching was not about what I knew; it was about how I could make an idea or a concept understandable for my students. I reworked that series of lessons, breaking down ideas into manageable pieces, and finally they understood.

There were only two girls in that class. Unfortunately, after the first week, one of the girls dropped out because she felt that the boys were much smarter than her (they were not). The remaining girl stayed at the back of the room and rarely spoke. I admired her bravery and encouraged her to voice her opinions, and she gained a feeling of strength through that experience. After I had taught at Vanier for twenty-six years, at last females made up at least half the students in the mathematics classes and half the teachers in the department.

I learned that if you could touch the heart of a student, you could teach them anything. I never met a student who wanted to fail my course. Their energy was infectious. They rose to the challenge of the subject because I believed in them. I think that many people do not see the passion teachers have and the dedication they bring not only to their profession but also to the lives of those young people every day in the classroom. Teaching is most certainly a noble profession.

Very early on in my teaching, I discovered that teenagers are most motivated by food. They always seem to be hungry. Perhaps the wealth of outdoor sports in the valley contributed to this constant need to eat. I developed something called "fridge formulas." I told my students to take down the elementary school art on their refrigerators and replace it with trigonometric identities or derivative formulas. I knew that they would constantly go to the fridge to check out what was inside in the hope that something new would magically appear (they actually live in hope). Their homework was to look at the formulas before opening the door, and then glance at them again while munching. Before long, they had everything memorized. I also developed "edible lessons." Early in the morning before class, I would rush across the Fifth Street Bridge before the traffic got too bad (the Seventeenth Street Bridge was not a reality yet) and purchase a plump watermelon from Safeway. When I cut each slice, my hungry students could see the cylindrical shapes. As each piece dripped in their hands and mouths, they understood that the sum of all these slices provided the development for the new definite integration formula that determined the volume of a solid of rotation.

I began holding calculus retreats at my home. If you could have retreats for music or basketball, why couldn't you have one devoted to calculus? Having several classes of my students in one room, discussing the "big ideas" of the Advanced Placement Calculus course, not only prepared them for their external examination in May, but also was enjoyable. Even with all the tempting outdoor activities of the Comox Valley, these young students came to a calculus retreat and had fun. Calculus beats skiing! By providing food and a co-operative environment for them to work together, discuss ideas and get feedback from me and from each other, they saw the big picture and experienced a co-operative immersion that was of great benefit.

As a feminist, I read books such as *Our Bodies, Ourselves*, like so many of my women friends at that time. In the early seventies at a women's retreat in Tlell, I realized that sometimes I was different in my approach to things. Each woman was asked to create an individual sign about something she loved, such as the ocean, trees, flowers and so forth. My sign said, "I love my calculator." As you can imagine, not many people wanted to talk to me or understood that I was indeed serious about that statement. I actually do love technology, and my calculator opened doors that were not possible before. When I wrote my scholarship examination in grade 12 in Terrace, I had to use a slide rule as well as trigonometric and logarithmic tables. Now, with one simple keystroke, I could find values that were previously cumbersome to determine and at times could only be

"Let the sunshine in." I am enjoying the warmth of Kye Bay, most likely thinking mathematical thoughts—or maybe not.

approximated through interpolation. My affection for calculators only got stronger as technology improved to include the use of graphing calculators.

Balancing teaching, being a mathematics department head, being a mother of two young children, being a wife and finding time for myself was challenging. The only time I could find to walk around Crown Isle Golf Course with my three good friends was from 6 to 7 a.m. I saw the men in the staff room with their neatly packed lunches in little containers, prepared by their wives at home, and I felt that I wanted a "wife" for myself. However, when I consider what so many other women had to do in much tougher times, we had it very easy.

All things must change. Roger and I were ending our married life; we parted as friends and we remained close to one another for many years. I left the valley in 2002 for a new teaching position at St. Michaels University School. I came to SMUS for one year and stayed for nine, first as the Hinton chair of mathematics and then as the head of mathematics. I remember driving down Island when I went for the interview for that job. I couldn't really believe I was doing this, since I adored Vanier and didn't think I would ever leave the Comox Valley, which was my home, but I did.

The natural beauty of the Comox Valley and the beauty of the community nurtured the artistry I developed in my teaching and in my artwork. In 2004 I started creating wearable art using silver and copper. Experiencing the talented local silver artists in the valley led me to become a silver artist. I am inspired by the sea life and nature of the valley and in Victoria. Mussels collected by my friend Lynda from Tree Island and logarithmic spirals found in shells from Hornby and Denman Islands, as well as sunflowers from gardens around our home, provide sources of inspiration. My mathematical background also influences the distinct designs in my drawings and etchings; circles and spirals feature in many of my pieces of jewellery. I have been chosen to be an artisan in the Filberg Festival over the past few years, so I return to the Comox Valley with my new husband, Bindon, whom I was fortunate to meet in 2008. I visit old friends, students and the beautiful valley that I called home for so many years. I am able to see the Comox Valley through mature eyes and realize the value of my time there. How magical it is to come back to visit and to be involved in something I love.

As Joni Mitchell sang, over the years I have had losses and gains, but in my present life I am blessed with creativity, love, friends and family. The longer I live, the more I am thankful for those formative years spent in the beauty and comfort of the Comox Valley.

Beyond the Valley

BRENDA DEMPSEY
Arrived in 1976

The date for our departure had been decided. Our small fourteen-foot lapstrake boat, the Marisol, converted to sail with leeboards, was painted and ready. The sails were set, our gear stowed as safely as possible. Our white cat, Kipper, and springer spaniel, Seadog, were on board. As I looked out to sea, the clouds rolled in, threatening rain: a summer southeaster was moving down the Strait of Juan de Fuca. All our friends from Sombrio Beach on the west coast of Vancouver Island were on the beach to see us off and to help roll the boat into the water. Roger carefully guided us through the razor-toothed rocks and we set sail. Immediately, the wind picked up and huge swells roared under our tiny boat. I had only known this man, with his long blond ringlets and twinkly blue sailor eyes, for five months. Was he capable of taking us through this maelstrom? I had moved from the relative civility of Ottawa and the Gatineau Lake area the year before, and I was uncertain about this wild West Coast experience. Instead of going north, we turned back toward Victoria, and the little craft surfed down the waves. I was terrified and exhilarated at the same time. Suddenly, the rudder broke and we had no way to guide our boat. Roger quickly downed the mainsail, and with a little jib sheet and an oar, he skilfully guided us into the calm of Jordan River.

We spent that first summer together on the boat, exploring the islands and bays and sailing the straits of Barkley Sound. As summer closed, we trailered the boat over to Parksville, as Roger had friends from Barrie, Ontario, who were also living on a boat in Campbell River.

We arrived in Campbell River in the fall of 1974, enthused by this gypsy lifestyle. With little money but excited by the options available on the east coast, we immediately set to work on our dream of living on and around the small islands with no ferry access or roads.

Roger had experience painting boats in Barrie, so we painted our truck and picked up small painting jobs around the Campbell River dock. We found a caretaking job that winter and the following summer in Quartz Bay, on Cortes Island. We loved the lifestyle: fresh fish, clams and oysters just outside our front door and a small garden for greens. We enjoyed many dances at the Gorge Hall on Cortes and made many coastal friends who shared our relish of the back-to-the-land movement and enjoyment of the Salish Sea. Unfortunately, our cabin in Quartz Bay burned down that spring; we quickly relocated to Campbell River, with the idea of making enough money to move to the outer islands.

Through folks from Black Creek, we found a trailer on a lot on Mac-Caulay Road, not far from the racetrack. With our truck, Roger and I turned up every day to different houses around the area to put up siding. We even took a job laying carpets. However, our first love was the water, and we still visited friends on islands along the east coast of the Island as often as possible. Finally, we found a job at Bennett's Point at Gourmet by the Sea, running their tackle shop and guiding fishing trips. This work suited us better. I looked after the tackle shop and booked the fishing trips. Roger was the guide, and as he loved fishing and boats, it was a perfect fit. I was pregnant that summer of 1977, but I found the work interesting. Launching the boat down the steep ramp was tricky but fun. On our little lot on MacCaulay, we started homesteading, roughing out a small garden. We picked up a milking goat from friends in Coombs and a few chickens, ducks and geese. We would take the truck with Seadog and our goat, Circe, down to the nearby beaches for walks and seaweed picking. We considered buying property on MacCaulay, but instead Roger purchased a forty-foot former fishing boat and had it trailered to our place. Our goal was to re-build it to live aboard. However, the dream was bigger than our skill level, and the boat languished in the yard after he discovered a lot of rot in the planks and ribs.

We created a sweet community in Black Creek. We became friendly with a young French-Canadian couple, and we helped each other out with firewood and chores on the property. Lucille was pregnant as well, and it was good to have a friend to share the experience. Our friends Colin and Denise Nadeau up the road were also expecting a child, and we shared information and baby clothes. Three brothers farther up the road provided work in the off-season and big potluck parties in their roughed-in new home.

Roger and me spending Christmas in our trailer in Black Creek, 1975.

While attending a town hall meeting at the Merville Community Centre, we became involved in the fight against BC Hydro, which planned to spray the herbicide 2,4-D along the transmission lines. Both Denise and I educated ourselves on the hazards of 2,4-D and took an evening to drive up to Gold River to talk to the locals there about their concerns. Finally, BC Hydro backed off and the transmission lines were cut by hand, and

Roger and me with baby Elysia at the boat ways on Read Island, 1978.

the more targeted hack-and-squirt method for spreading the herbicide was used instead of aerial spraying.

I had been taking birthing classes on Headquarters Road; the pregnancy was giving me incentive to live a healthier lifestyle. We bought organic food at the new Fed-Up Co-op and went to the Comox Valley Sports Centre in Courtenay to swim regularly. Because of living in Black Creek, we opted for a birth in the hospital in Comox with Doctor Don, who attended many of the births in the valley. Nature had other plans.

I woke in the early hours of January 28, 1978, with a lurch and a large contraction. Even though we had a bag packed, it took us an hour or so to get ready. By the time I was in the van on a bed that Roger had set up in the back, I was in transition. Snow had fallen during the night and there were snowbanks all along the Island Highway. As we approached the hill into Courtenay, I realized the baby would not wait for us to make it to the hospital. I told Roger to pull over as the baby crowned. He was able to pull over at Pilon Tool Rentals at the bottom of the Courtenay hill. It was there, as he pulled open the van doors, that I birthed our baby, Elysia Coral. She was perfect and pink, just giving a little cry as we wrapped her in a blanket and drove to a friend's who was anticipating a home birth. Sally came out and cut the umbilical cord, and then we proceeded to the hospital, where

Doctor Don was on duty. After a quick checkup, we were on our way home with our sweet bundle. It was the perfect roadside birth!

The rest of the winter, we enjoyed our new baby, as we were not working much. It was a relaxing time to explore motherhood. By May we were back working, booking fishing trips and guiding at Bennett's Point. Elysia stayed with me in a backpack, or my friend Joelle would take her for an hour or two when we were busy. That year, Gourmet by the Sea subcontracted the work out to a couple from Alberta. Everything was going along well until the end of the season. Suddenly, the contractors packed up in a hurry, gave Roger his last paycheque and disappeared. Of course the cheque bounced. With that betrayal, we were facing the winter with a lack of funds. Our dream of buying land on an island was in jeopardy.

However, by November 1979 we heard that a large floathouse was for sale in Loughborough Inlet. The price was right, and our friend Greg offered to tow it down for us with his log salvage boat, the *Hey Jude*. Roger went with Greg and they towed it down to Whiterock Pass on Maurelle Island. We moved out of the trailer by December, and Elysia was just eleven months old when we tied up the floathouse in a small bay on Read Island near our good friends Greg and Wendy. Roger picked up some guiding at the Big Bay Resort on Stuart Island that spring, and we were set to begin our new lives on the Discovery Islands coast.

In 1979 we ended up purchasing 147 acres of waterfront land on Read Island with six other families and one single man. We raised twelve beautiful children on the property. We built our own homes from wood milled from logs we salvaged, planted gardens and orchards and invested in solar panels and micro hydro systems. We danced and played and worked hard. We harvested our own food from the ocean and land.

For us the Comox Valley was a stepping stone to the adventures of an off-the-grid, boat-access lifestyle, but the Comox Valley has also always been our backyard. We held big community and school ski trips every winter, first at Forbidden Plateau and then at Mount Washington. In the summers, I took my and friends' children hiking and camping in the stunning Strathcona Provincial Park. Summers brought the Renaissance Fair and, later, the Comox Valley Music Festival. I can see Mount Albert Edward and Kings Peak, in Strathcona Park, from my front deck on Read Island.

My interests turned from homesteading to other pursuits. In the eighties, I began taking workshops at Hollyhock, a well-known retreat centre on Cortes Island. I studied with Starhawk, and my eyes opened to radical feminism and the sacredness of our connection to Mother Earth. I began studying with various teachers and became an acupressure therapist and a yoga and meditation teacher. Since 1990 I've supported myself by teaching retreats in meditation, yoga and qigong and practising energetic healing and acupressure. I feel that working with people to increase balance and wholeness within themselves helps balance the energies of our planet. This work has been satisfying and has given me a sense of peace and well-being. I've taught many classes in the Comox Valley, and many students from the valley have come to my retreats on Read Island and in Mexico.

I now spend five months a year in Mexico or travelling while teaching. At home I concentrate my healing practice to two days a week, and I also teach at small retreats at our homestead on Read Island. Many young people come through our place to experience an off-the-grid lifestyle and go deeper into their practice. It gives me great satisfaction to see the devotion these young folks have to living in harmony with nature. I find like-minded people all over this planet who are giving back. It gives me hope for the future that so many are involved in healing. Whether picking up trash on the beach, helping with educational programs, promoting human rights and freedoms or developing better management of our oceans, I feel the ideals that we brought in our back-to-the-land and love-of-nature movements are having a profound effect on this planet. Those ideals provide a balancing force to the prevalent destructive energy, which provides me with hope for a better future for our children and grandchildren. What more can I ask for? I feel blessed and fortunate to have such a diverse and interesting life, and that I can use my energies to effect change within myself and others. And so the dance of life and love continues.

All My Relations

GLORIA SIMPSON
Arrived in 1976

I was lucky to land here in the Comox Valley. When I came to Cumberland in the spring of 1976 at the age of twenty-seven, I had been on the move for most of my life. I had a son who would start school in the next year, and I needed to settle down for his sake and give him the stability of a secure place in a community.

I was born in the Yukon in 1948, the youngest child in a family of six children. My father was of mixed Tahltan native and Scottish immigrant descent, and grew up in Telegraph Creek, a small Tahltan village on the Stikine River in northern BC. My mother was of Irish descent, from early immigrants to West Virginia. Her family moved to the Peace River Country to homestead when she was four.

My parents decided not to stay and raise children in Telegraph Creek. The culture had been mostly shattered by colonialism, and the one-room school offered a very poor education. They bought one of the original US Army construction camps that had been used to build the Alaska Highway during World War Two, and they ran a roadside lodge on the Alaska Highway: a combination of hotel, café, gas station, garage and bar.

The lodge was remote, two hundred miles from Whitehorse, the Yukon's only town. When we kids were young, we developed a strong attachment to the land and spent all of our time outdoors playing together. The family hunted for all the meat we ate, picked berries, preserved food, camped and explored the land, boated, swam and fished in the lakes and rivers.

But there was no school nearby, so from the time I was five, my siblings and I were sent away for ten months out of the year to go to school. The longest time in one school was two years. We went to every different living situation imaginable, from Catholic and Anglican school residences to boarding with various types of families, an upper-class English-style boarding school and a prairie Lutheran school. We were exposed to every stripe of Christianity and many different lifestyles. After a while, none of them rang true. We were set adrift. By the time each of us turned twelve, when we went home for the summer, we worked in the family business. Our parents were run off their feet, working to provide for and educate six kids.

I did very well in school. I skipped a grade and ended up at the Univeristy of British Columbia at age seventeen. I took Timothy Leary's advice to "turn on, tune in and drop out." I became involved in the New Left and dropped out of university in second year. I lived with a radical and charismatic Dutch man, Paul, who was thirteen years older than me, and we had a son, Oti, in 1970. For years, we lived a nomadic life, with a seasonal circuit: Mexico to northern California to Vancouver to the Ottawa Valley, living mostly in rural communal situations. We lived in a converted school bus, a tipi, a geodesic dome, a tree house and a modified Mendocino water tower. It was a kind of Cook's tour of counterculture: the Zen commune, the SDS (Students for a Democratic Society) commune, the pottery commune and the Renaissance Craft Fair farm commune. We worked with the SDS and the Black Panthers, and in the anti-Vietnam-War and free-speech movements in San Diego and in Berkeley. In the Ottawa Valley, we organized big craft fairs in the summers.

Eventually, Paul spent time in jail in California for possession of marijuana and the manufacture and possession of firebombs. When he got out, he had changed. Over the next two years, our relationship broke down, so I found myself looking for a new way to get on, alone with my six-year-old son. I wanted to live in a small village in BC, on the coast. Cumberland was recommended to me by friends in Vancouver as a place with very low house prices. It happened that Roland, one of Paul's brothers, was living in Cumberland with his wife and two children, so I stayed with them for a while, and then rented a small, dumpy house.

Cumberland then was very quiet and rundown. The last of the coal mines had closed about ten years earlier, and the population of the town had been shrinking. The town was impoverished, but it had many amenities left from when it was a booming company town: good schools, a recreation centre, a pharmacy and a health centre. It had its own water system, with the water rights to five lakes above the town, and the drinking water was delicious. There was a village park and a beach park at the lake close by. There were lots of empty lots, some empty houses, and house prices were very low. People in the district scorned Cumberland for being economically depressed and rough, but I soon came to know that it was in fact a place with a huge heart. It had an illustrious history in the labour movement, and many of the residents had lived here for generations. The solidarity in the community was very comforting: to me it felt tribal. We were newcomers, but these working-class, historically socialist people were very tolerant and inclined to leave us alone to live as we liked. We had a lot in common: growing gardens, making wine, getting firewood for our wood stoves and hanging the laundry on clotheslines to dry. This is a town where kids go out to play, walk to school or their friends' houses or the lake or the forest, ride bikes and explore and spend summer days swimming. It was exactly what I was looking for.

Cumberland is nestled in the foothills of the Beaufort Range and was then still surrounded by big second-growth Douglas fir forests. Through these forests run old railbeds and overgrown logging roads, so I could walk for hours in the woods in beauty and solitude. Comox Lake was within walking distance, and there were beaches and creeks that could be reached by lovely, private trails. Around town were old abandoned orchards and gardens where I could pick fruit and flowers. I decided to stay.

That summer I made friends with a larger and larger group of new-comers to the valley. Boudewijn, another of Paul's brothers, moved to the valley with his friend Jon, who became my lover. Jeanine, a Dutch immi-grant whom I had met before in Ontario and Vancouver, moved to Cum-berland and we became friends. That fall, Jeanine and I rented a big Victo-rian house in the same block as Roland. Jeremy, an acquaintance from my time in Roberts Creek, also moved in with us.

Jeanine, Jeremy and I enjoyed sharing a house. We grew a big garden, ate a lot of our own veggies and fruit and canned a huge amount of food in the fall. We shared with little friction; all three of us cooked and cleaned. A lot of visitors stayed with us, and we cooked up enormous feasts, including a Christmas dinner for about twenty-five friends. Jeremy and Jeanine were both good to my son, supportive in every way, even helping financially by splitting expenses three ways instead of charging me extra for Oti. When Jeanine and I went away to plant trees the next spring, Jeremy cared for Oti, even putting on a big birthday party with a piñata. They had a series of professional photos taken of Oti and framed them as a birthday gift for me. Their kindness made such a difference in my life and Oti's.

Jeanine and I wanted to be hired by the Westwind tree-planting com-pany, but at that time reforestation was considered "man's work." The com-pany was owned by a group of experienced, high-production young men

Ready to leave the landing. Such steep, slashy slopes above Comox Lake; such heavy planting bags full of mud-packed seedlings. We had to laugh! Photo Jane Gilchrist

Feeding friends in my old miner's shack the day we took a chainsaw to the back wall and then kicked it out. Another happy work party. Photo Eileen Bennett

who doubted that women were capable of doing the job. They did, however, give us a contract they didn't want, picking conifer cones for Crown Zellerbach, up on Mount Washington before the ski resort was developed. We worked for the head forester, John, another Dutch immigrant who became a good friend. The logging company was clear-cutting high-elevation virgin timber and needed tree seed from that specific microclimate for successful reforestation. Twelve young local women newcomers worked together. John had us set up an old wringer washer on the landing, and we ran chopped-up hemlock branches through the wringer to pop the little cones off into a bin: we called ourselves the "wringer crew." We worked beside a nice, big bonfire and had a good time and lots of laughs. One of the women, Paulette, had a Texas drawl, and she would yell out, "Branches! Branches!" to urge us on. Of course, for years after, we called her Branches and only let up when she became a practising Adlerian psychologist. Danny, an ex-faller who worked on John's forestry crew, was the only man working with us. He kept everything running smoothly, felling and limbing the chosen trees and feeding the fire. We were lucky to have him; he was so cheerful, friendly and capable.

While we were working, a group of people went into the woods, reappearing a few hours later with big baskets full of pine mushrooms (*matsutake*) to sell for the Japanese market. After asking them about it, we went mushroom hunting during our lunch hour. I took the pines to Campbell River to a buyer that weekend and learned more about how to find them and what to pick. I was interested in mycology and had gathered for the table for years. For the next thirty years, every fall I picked both chanterelles and pines commercially; I was often in the woods all day exploring, with a compass to find my way back. I built up knowledge of where the pines grew, areas that produced every year and could be picked every ten days during the season, if I was careful not to disturb the forest floor. The young "button" stage was the most valuable, worth up to a hundred dollars a pound early in the season, so the load wasn't heavy, and the daily cash made for a good supplemental income. The forest in the fall is beautiful, bright and open, and the best attitude for hunting mushrooms is meditative and Zenlike.

Oti started school in Cumberland the fall after we arrived. At first the local kids tried to tease him about his clothes, his hand-spun, natural-dyed sweater and leatherworker-made shoes, and his lunches of homemade brown bread and sprouts. Oti soon got through that phase, with the help of his cousins and the neighbours he'd befriended over the summer. He was gentle and sensitive but also smart and rational. He had lived communally with many people and travelled widely; he wasn't easily intimidated. I won't deny that he may have had to win a fight to establish himself in the boys' pecking order. Soon he was friends with many "old-time Cumberland" kids. During that first year, Oti didn't enjoy school, finding it too restrictive and boring, so I didn't insist he go every day. The school protested, but we held our ground. In grade 2, the school tested him, and finding out how bright he is, they put him in a program for gifted children, with a wonderful teacher. The same group of children studied together under her tutelage all through elementary school. Oti enjoyed school and became lifelong friends with those students.

I was also involved in midwifery, having studied in California, and I delivered babies there and in the Ottawa Valley. In the seventies in BC, midwifery wasn't legal. No training was available in Canada, nor were any of the equipment, supplies and drugs that should be on hand. If things went wrong there was no backup, no doctor coming to the house, no taking the woman to the hospital and continuing to attend her there. If mother or baby suffered "a bad outcome," the midwife could expect to be charged with practising medicine without a licence, perhaps even charged with manslaughter, perhaps go to jail. Still, women were adamant in wanting home delivery, because they wanted more control of the birth experience and not to be subjected to the standard practices in hospitals at that time: authoritarian rules, episiotomies, drugging and sometimes possibly unnecessary Caesarean sections. If a pregnant woman had prenatal care from a doctor, was considered to be at low risk of complication and understood the risk, I would attend. I delivered three babies here in the valley, some with a friendly young local doctor present for backup, and they were a joy. Denise Nadeau was one of the friends that I attended. I feel a certain bond with these women and their children.

The fourth birth that I helped with was on Denman Island, with Skye, a young woman who aspired to become a midwife and had asked me to help. We crossed the strait from Deep Bay on a fishboat, in the dark of the wee hours of the morning. Once we arrived at the woman's home, I was not comfortable with the situation: lots of people, low light, loud drumming. All went well until mid-morning, when suddenly I felt that we were in big trouble. Skye was keen to catch the baby, but after delivering the head, I found that the baby's position was difficult. We were able to manipulate and successfully deliver, but the baby was a terrifying blue. We quickly revived her, but then the mother began to hemorrhage and the placenta wouldn't deliver. We called the local doctor, a woman, who came and stopped the bleeding with Pitocin (a drug not available to us midwives) and with Skye's help completed the afterbirth. Skye and I were debriefed by doctors and we were deemed to be not at fault. The mother and baby did well. I did not. This event brought home to me the unpredictable, immediate life-and-death reality of childbirth. I considered it a wake-up call, thought I was guilty of hubris and never again practised midwifery. Skye, on the other hand, went on through medical school to a doctor's practice. I am very happy that midwifery is now an accepted and supported part of medicine in BC, and that hospitals have also much improved their handling of births.

In the spring of 1977, Jeanine and I finally got jobs tree planting by signing on with a co-op, a start-up that hired newbies, and we did two camping-out contracts: in Bute Inlet and around Harrison Lake. It was a gong show and we made very little money, but we did learn to plant.

That fall and for two falls after, John, the Crown Zellerbach forester, hired Jeanine and me to do forestry tech work. We did good work, so John gave us the local tree-planting contracts, the plum contracts that Westwind had before then. We agreed to hire the Westwind men if they would hire us for other contracts they had later in the season. Within a year, I was one of the highest-producing workers, and over the years I planted well over a million trees. I worked for that company for twenty years, mostly as a contractor or foreman. The company hired more women, and eventually the numbers of men and women balanced. I became an industrial first-aid attendant in charge of our safety program and worked on the Workers' Compensation Board committee that wrote the new regulations governing tree-planting camps. I also instigated the company being certified in the International Woodworkers of America union.

When I went away to work, Oti lived with my close friend Eileen. She was brilliant, radical and multi-talented, and she laughed a lot. She lived in a big Victorian house with her handsome younger husband and her son, and they took in many children: Oti, foster kids and exchange students. Living with her was good for Oti.

The work enabled me to buy an old miner's shack on Camp Road in Cumberland. It was about seventy-five years old, decrepit, in need of renovation of everything from foundation to roof, but it had a huge yard, was on the sunny side of a dead-end street and the backyard bordered on forest. I needed a lot of help to come up with the price of fourteen thousand dollars. My brother signed as guarantor, and I applied for a first-time homebuyer's grant for the down payment. While waiting the very long time that grant took to be approved, I couldn't get bridge financing, and the frustrated realtor lent me his own money! Oti and I moved in and lived with the seemingly endless renovations. However, I have been happy there, and have ended up with a beautiful rebuilt house, with a nice suite, surrounded by terraced gardens, with long-standing neighbours I'm very fond of, some that moved here at my urging years ago.

Roots: A Story of Migration and Community

JEANINE MAARS
Arrived in 1976

Bute Inlet is one of the steepest fjords in BC. The inlet extends seventy-five kilometres north into the glaciated mountain wilderness of the province's mainland. The views over the milky green water are spectacular.

I was there to plant trees, new to tree planting and relatively new to the country. I was drinking in all this beauty, as you would expect from someone coming here from a country that lies largely below sea level, where the highest point is about one thousand feet. At age twenty-two, I immigrated to Canada from the Netherlands, drawn by adventure, possibilities and the beautiful vastness of this country. Vancouver Island was my landing spot. The Island is about 84 percent of the size of the Netherlands. In 1976 the population of Vancouver Island was 441,000; the population of the Netherlands was 13.7 million. The difference in topography is also great: the Netherlands is flat, cultivated and ordered; Vancouver Island is mountainous, treed and wild. I was contemplating this stark contrast as I looked up at the steep slope above me.

One of my fellow planters told me to just go up in a straight line to the top of the run, keeping a certain amount of spacing between trees and rows, alongside other planters. Easier said than done: my line started with an enormous boulder at the bottom, and I encountered mainly rock all the way up. I made it to the top though, a major feat in seriously steep terrain. And while I stood there puffing and congratulating myself that I made it, the planter next to me asked how many trees I had managed to plant. So busy struggling up that cliff, I had not planted a single tree. That was inexperience, all right! I was a person in unknown terrain.

My parents had both followed a similar path. My father left Holland for Venezuela right after World War Two, with a suitcase, a degree and a job offer. My mother, always a gutsy adventurer, followed him a year later. They left everything that was familiar to them for an unknown country and life together. What I remember of all their stories is that they loved their new life. Freedom from the deprivations and devastation of the war prompted their departure from Holland, and the freedom to be young and carefree kept them in Venezuela. I was born in my parents' adopted country, as were my three brothers and three sisters. The untimely death of my father forced my mother back to the Netherlands after fourteen years in Venezuela, back to a society she knew, but also didn't recognize. I wondered if they had felt some of the hesitation I now felt about moving to an unfamiliar country far away from family.

I lived in the Netherlands since grade 6 and graduated from high school with a scholarship to go to university in the US. Before I arrived in Minnesota and again after I left there, I travelled extensively through the western and eastern parts of Canada and the US. I was stunned by the vastness of these two countries and their natural beauty.

The late sixties were politically charged times in the US. I couldn't help but become involved with the Vietnam War draft resisters and the Poor People's Campaign in Minneapolis. I realized that not only was there so much physical space here, there was also space to become involved in what my heart was drawn to. On this continent I could shake off the constriction of European society and have freedom from class and academic expectations. Was I becoming an activist and a rebel? Not really; this all felt very natural to me, as if it was in my genes.

I spent my first years in Canada on the west coast of Vancouver Island and briefly in Ontario. When my marriage there ended, I fled back to the welcoming West Coast, with its relaxed way of life. I knew a couple who lived in the Comox Valley, and I decided to head there at the beginning of 1976. What was evident to me right away was the diversity of people living in the valley. Artists, health professionals, ex-miners, mill workers, educators, musicians, military people, draft dodgers, forestry workers, fishers, adventurers, hippies, hermits and seekers: so many had moved here from elsewhere. It made me feel that I had come home to something familiar.

Those first months I volunteered a lot and was of service to people I met. I tried some new things, such as splitting cedar shakes for a roof and doing a brake job on an old Bedford van. A regular meeting place in the valley was the Arts Alliance on McPhee Avenue. I spent many hours there.

Contemplating becoming Canadian. Photo Ed Robertson

Gallery shows, movies, concerts, dances and good food brought people to-gether. There were lots of opportunities to volunteer, as the place was run on grant money. I remember sewing hundreds of feet of burlap together to make wall coverings for this enormous space. It was also the place where I first heard about tree planting. This really appealed to me and I decided I wanted to try it. How Canadian is that? I wanted to plant with a local reforestation company that had a very good reputation, but I was told that they didn't hire women and certainly not inexperienced ones. It was with some annoyance that I saw inexperienced male friends leave to work with this company.

However, Gloria Simpson and I were asked to take over a local cone-picking contract of theirs. John was the local forester managing the job, and meeting him proved to be a stroke of good fortune. Cone picking is a rather sedentary job. Once the faller took down the chosen tree, we sat amongst the branches and picked off the cones. It was a tedious and daunting task to fill a burlap sack with small hemlock cones the size of a dime. It was great to be outside and in the mountains, but it was very cold work at times. We would make large fires to keep warm. Determined to get experience tree planting, Gloria and I signed on with a crew based on Denman Island. Our first contract was in Bute Inlet. Before we left to go there, we helped our cook, Emma, shop for food for twenty to thirty people for a month. The amounts were staggering: a hundred dozen eggs? We left in early March, after loading trucks, a bus, all our supplies and ourselves onto a barge, and headed up the inlet.

The first order of business once we arrived was to build a bear-proof storage for all our food supplies. This was all pretty exciting and a little intimidating, as we were unsure that we would really be able to keep the grizzly bears away from our food. We would soon learn that Emma's delicious meals and the warm cookshack at the end of the day made us forget the trials of the day and sometimes the night. I remember waking up very confused early one morning in my tent, not quite sure where I was. An unexpected snowfall during the night had collapsed several of our tents, including mine. Getting up and out was the first major challenge of that day.

Gloria Simpson and I ran our own contracts with Crown Zellerbach. Photo Jane Gilchrist, taken in the mountains above Comox Lake.

Heading to the sauna after a day of planting was a most welcome activity. After we built the bear-proof storage, we built a sauna, a frame structure covered in plastic with a wood stove inside. We warmed up in the sauna, then "washed" in the fast-flowing icy river and fled back into the sauna to warm up again. My kayaking buddies of today, who think I am a cold-water wimp, should have known me then!

Fortunately, I soon got the hang of planting trees and managing to find those little pockets of soil. My body gradually adjusted to the challenges, and I loved the hard physical labour and the feeling of being so strong and fit.

Only a few years earlier, both my parents' expectations and my own success in school had led me down an academic path in Europe. I hadn't wanted to follow that path. The majestic beauty of nature, the freedom to explore and the endless opportunities I saw in the US and Canada made one thing clear to me: this felt more like home. It also felt really good planting trees in these logged areas and contributing to rebuilding the beauty of the mountains.

While home in Cumberland between contracts, we planted our extensive vegetable gardens before moving to contracts in the Interior of BC. From the steep coastal mountains, we moved to easier terrain with gentler slopes close to quiet lakes and streams. Here the tally of how many trees we planted in a day increased dramatically. I planted with this supposedly co-operatively run company all spring, but I was unhappy about their financial arrangements and looking to making a change. By that fall Gloria and I were running our own contracts with John. He was very impressed by our meticulous work, and that he and I are both Dutch strengthened our relationship. We also ended up doing annual forestry surveys for him, calculating lengths and diameters of trees and survival rates. I really enjoyed that work, feeling that these surveys would improve both planting methods and survival rates. Planting from our home base in Cumberland was a cream contract. Home every night to running water and a warm bed!

I loved the tree-planting lifestyle, with its periods of hard physical work in the spring and fall and lots of time off in the summer and winter. No matter how much I enjoyed tree planting, though, there were bad days. Days with so much snow that no matter what I wore or how I layered, I got very cold and soaked. All I could think about was walking down the mountain, going home and never coming back. The weather was particularly brutal on my birthday one year. I had absolutely reached my limit of cold misery and physical discomfort. I am sure I scared the crew by sitting down, crying and begging to go home. When Gloria pulled out a bottle of champagne to celebrate my birthday, it warmed my heart if nothing else.

Sometimes I planted in areas where the lichen grew abundant and long on the vegetation around. It stuck to my hands and face and I couldn't get rid of it, no matter how much I tried to shake it off. It felt like one of the tortures of Tantalus. Or in the fall, when the six-foot-high fireweed set seed, I had the fluff in my ears, eyes and up my nose. Everyone on the crew looked like guerrilla warriors planting, trying to protect ourselves from the seed invasion, all the while sneezing and wheezing. Over the years, I put a dibble or a mattock into BC soil so many times I felt like I too was taking root here.

I applied for Canadian citizenship, the third citizenship in my life. I wished I could apply to be a "world" citizen, not defined by a single country. But choosing to become a Canadian was the next best choice for me, not dictated by accidental place of birth or birth parents. The valley felt like home to me now. A place where I found a community of people from very diverse backgrounds and a variety of people I could connect with. I even began to think about starting my own family.

Both of my daughters were born in the Comox Valley, and whether their roots will be in BC or elsewhere is their choice. Growing up here, they experienced the many different groups and communities we became part of. They have had parents and grandparents with a sense of adventure, courage and curiosity, who followed their hearts. All of this will serve them well in their lives.

More than forty years later, I continue to have a deep connection with my siblings in Europe. When I am there, I feel very much a Canadian. And when I am in Canada, I feel that I am Dutch too. I still live in the Comox Valley, now in an amazing co-housing community where my grandchildren love to come and visit. I had always felt that I was different when I lived in Venezuela. I knew I didn't really belong there. Later, when I moved to Holland, I felt unique there too because of my experience of living in Venezuela and travelling with my parents to different continents. I felt a belonging in the Comox Valley with like-minded people with causes and passions and an opportunity for limitless possibilities. I settled and set down roots.

A Shared Journey

Marguerite Masson
Arrived in 1977

The year 1978 was special for many reasons. I graduated with a B.Ed. from the University of Calgary. Stan and I were married. I became pregnant with our daughter, Rebecca. We settled in the Comox Valley. Yes, 1978 was certainly special.

I first came to the valley in the summer of 1977 and worked for the Courtenay Recreational Association for three months, helping to organize and implement the outdoor camps, day trips and overnights for children. What a fantastic job! It gave me the opportunity to discover and explore the Comox Valley as well as the surrounding areas. The seed of settling in the valley was planted.

When Stan and I met in Mexico, while both travelling solo, we had deep conversations on how we wanted to lead our lives. We agreed to be independent, live in the present, have children that would adapt to our lifestyle, and lead healthy, outdoorsy lives. We were young. If being told that we were young implied that we were strong, healthy and willing to take on new challenges, we were proud. If it implied that we were naive, we were incensed. We were willing to work and play hard to achieve the lifestyle we dreamed of. We had both been to the Comox Valley, so it was an easy decision to choose this beautiful area, which offered both mountains and ocean, as our home base. Natural beauty, being able to experience healthy outdoor pursuits, and a safe environment for raising children were shared goals and important factors in choosing where to live.

After I completed my bachelor of education in Calgary, Stan and I travelled to Prince Edward Island, where we got married. We then travelled all the way back across the country, caravan-style. From PEI to Calgary, we drove a three-ton truck that carried a very few personal belongings, a Triumph motorcycle in pieces and a six-week-old kitten. We also pulled a very old and ugly but practical trailer, which was our home. In Calgary we added a 1954 Chevy pickup to our fleet and drove both trucks out to the coast, where we settled on my sister and brother-in-law's front lawn. Lucky them!

Being determined to make the Comox Valley our home, we quickly had to attend to the realities of life. We had arrived four months pregnant, jobless and homeless. It took only a few days before we both had jobs and a place to rent. I worked as a teacher on call for School District 71 as well as hostessing at the Old House Restaurant. Stan had worked for his brother in Ontario, installing aluminum siding, and with that experience he was able to pick up a job. Working at the Old House quickly became a huge part of our social life. It was a happening place. Friends gathered there to listen to local music and share good times, not to mention excellent food. Our rental house was on Hilton Road, close to the wrecks in Royston. It was a cute little place that we dearly wanted to buy, though we didn't have any money to do so. However, it was part of an estate shared by many grandchildren, and they weren't in agreement on whether or not to sell. Not wanting to rent, after about three or four months, we bought two acres on Rennie Road, ten kilometres north of Courtenay. The property cost sixteen thousand dollars, and the owner graciously carried the mortgage. It included a twenty-by-thirty-foot framed structure and an open dug well. I signed the papers in the hospital on the same day our daughter, Rebecca, was born.

We had a project! Stan, being a very independent twenty-three-year-old handyman, read the red electrical guidebook, as well as information on plumbing, and so was able to complete our little shack with the help of an unskilled labourer, namely me. We furnished it with items bought at the auction in Cumberland. One of the items was a bathtub, where Rebecca had her naps while we installed insulation, wiring, plumbing and Gyproc all around her. We moved in the month of March, I believe. It was at this time that my brother paid us a visit to welcome our new baby. His gift was not the most appropriate. It was a six-week-old, very active Lab cross puppy. Cute but... sad to say, the puppy played a little too hard with our cat, which had just given birth to kittens we had not yet found. We came home one day to find the puppy trying to revive the cat, which was dead. We were able to find the two-day-old kittens, but it was quite an ordeal to feed them with an eyedropper while trying to finish our shack and look after baby Rebecca.

Having the two acres was exactly what we had hoped for. After living in what appeared to be a war zone for several months, we did plant a small garden and got laying hens. The rest of the two acres were still very rough, with old stumps strewn around. I did the washing in an old wringer washer

Enjoying a peaceful moment with my daughter, Rebecca.

and dried the clothes, mostly diapers, on one of the many clotheslines we had strung in the wasteland.

When it was time to add on to our little shack, we built a log addition over two years, as we had the funds. The log house was another "learn as you go" project. Following Allan Mackie's log-house-building book, Stan learned to scribe the logs so they fit perfectly on top of each other. Getting up early in the morning, I would help him raise the next log into position using a winch and tackle. We hand-picked the river rocks for our fireplace. We split all the rails for the fencing. It was a lot of work, but it was what we wanted. By this time, I was working full-time, teaching French as a second language to grades 4 through 7 in three different schools. Stan had his own business installing siding. In the second year of building, we were also expecting our second child, Kyle. He spent the first six months of his life sleeping in an old English pram. It was perfect, as it served as both a stroller and a portable bed. He began crawling at four months, and we dreaded the day he would climb out of the pram, but he never did. It was ideal for wheeling him around to where I was landscaping or working at whatever was needed while his sister played with building materials and climbed ladders. Once she climbed to the roof and walked along the four-inch-wide strapping along the edge. It was a two-storey drop to either a cement floor or the ground. Luckily, her dad snuck up on her and rescued her.

Yeah! Our home is no longer a tarpaper shack and now displays a setting-sun design. Funky!

Upon completion of the log addition, we were able to divert our attention to enlarging the garden and clearing the debris to make pasture areas. While we were still in our tarpaper shack, we had chickens, but once we made pasture areas, we purchased a couple of pigs, a calf, rabbits and meat birds. What a haven for young children! This was again "learn as you go" for me but old hat for Stan, who grew up on a farm in southern Ontario. Raising and caring for animals was a unique experience for me. I had returned to the Old House Restaurant after Kyle was born, as teaching jobs became scarce. I welcomed the pigs' frenzied squealing as I drove home from work, as they knew I had slop buckets especially for them. However, it caught me completely off guard when, one day, I returned home with the kids to find the skins of two of our rabbits hanging from a clothesline! Stan figured they had escaped to cause havoc in the garden once too often. But hey, the kids and I thought of them as pets. The children were pretty little to be responsible for keeping the latch securely fastened.

We were never sure if we were true Mervillites, as we lived on the "other" side of the highway, but that didn't stop us from enjoying the social functions at the Merville Hall. The dances were a highlight for the whole family, as our children accompanied us and joined other young children who were put to bed in a corner of the dance hall. The Bickle movie theatre was also a hit, as we didn't own a television but could nevertheless enjoy movies from the family room at the back of the theatre. From there, we could watch the featured movie while our kids slept in a crib that could house several children.

Courtenay was a small town. When I went grocery shopping at Safeway, it would take longer than anticipated, as I inevitably met and visited with friends. The thrift store was also a meeting place, as was the nearby laundromat.

Over the years, we have lived in one more new home that we built and two homes that we renovated. Our goals are amazingly still very similar to our original goals. I continue to enjoy outdoor pursuits as well as a few indoor hobbies. I still get a feeling of accomplishment and satisfaction from doing yardwork and renovations. Our children have adopted some of our beliefs and also call the Comox Valley home, along with their children. For the past twenty-one years, we have lived close to our original little rental house. I feel fortunate and grateful for my life.

Back to What Land?

JUDY NORBURY
Arrived in 1977

Growing up in Vancouver, after coming from India at the age of four, I'd say I had a nearly perfect childhood. I had contracted polio in India, and when I was no longer critically ill our family relocated to Canada, the home of my mother. After a tortured year in the Vancouver Children's Hospital, I joined my mother, father and sister in a big old wood house my family bought in an east-side neighbourhood near my grandparents, aunties and cousins.

Both my parents were great story-tellers, particularly my father, who had left England at the age of eighteen and had spent the next twenty-three years in India working at a hand-knotted carpet company, one of many situated along the banks of the Ganges River. Not only would he tell us stories, he would also read to us; all the classics, such as *Treasure Island* and *Robinson Crusoe*, were on the list. We especially loved his Sunday afternoon readings of Sherlock Holmes. My mother sang beautifully and told us funny stories about her family and growing up during the Depression. She had joined my father in India in 1948 and I was born in 1949.

School, friends, family picnics and holidays, and a steady boyfriend from age fourteen, filled my time until I left home at nineteen. After my first digs, a basement suite, I moved into a large rented house, minus the boyfriend, this time on the west side of Vancouver with five good friends. Those were the days of anti-Vietnam-War protests, rock 'n' roll concerts, hashish and pot, playing songs on my newly acquired guitar and late-night conversations about how we would prepare for "when the system collapsed" and also "going back to the land." All but one of our households did just that. (Funny how we talked about "going back to the land" when none of us had ever lived on "the land" in the first place!)

Playing my J.R. Stone dulcimer and singing to the changing tides in the cabin on beautiful Oyster Bay. Photo Ruben Kaufman

After only eight months in that house—so many things happened during those eventful and exciting days that it seems like years in my memory—we all left in various pairings. I moved to Pender Harbour on the Sunshine Coast, accessed by ferry, with one of my housemates, Doug, who had become my boyfriend. His father had purchased seventeen acres of land, which consisted of a beautiful tidal flat, creek and forest at the headwaters of Pender Harbour, locally known as Oyster Bay. It was there that I experienced my first great blue heron. It looked like a pterodactyl as it rose from the swamp, making ungodly raucous croaks…I was stunned. Also new to me were the majestic, trilling bald eagles, at that time on the endangered list, and ravens and their multitude of calls, croaks and clicks. I also learned rampant new plants: salal, Oregon grape, wild columbine and wild strawberries.

We camped on the site while we built a cabin. I say we, but it was really Doug who did the building, as I use a wheelchair. If the tide was in, we came in by rowboat, and if it was out, I was piggybacked a quarter mile through a field and forest. Doug's father was also building a cabin on what we called the "Island," a part of the property that became an island at high tide. His vehicle brought in supplies for both building projects. I did the cooking and washing up for the three of us while the building progressed. Doug built the floor and roof and we set up our household. He built the rest of the cabin around us. Water was collected in buckets from the roof for washing and from the creek for cooking and drinking. Kerosene, candles and a Coleman stove took the place of electricity, and we heated with a tin airtight stove, cheap and ubiquitous in cabins during those days.

After three years of fairly isolated living and a desire to explore other relationships, Doug and I went our separate ways quite amicably, and I continued to live in the cabin when I wasn't travelling. I made arrangements with friends and visitors to come and go. If I wasn't able to wrangle a ride, I'd hitchhike to Vancouver. There always seemed to be someone to house-sit and stay with my lovely malamute shepherd dog, Lakshmi, and if not, she would come with me. As well as travelling to Vancouver and Vancouver Island, I made some forays into the BC Interior and five trips to California.

In my periods of solitude at the cabin, and there were many, the longest being eighteen days, I played music on my beloved Appalachian dulcimer. It was built by J.R. Stone, a truly gifted instrument builder who lived in a house across the bay. During those solitary times I began to write songs. I had friends from Pender Harbour who had moved to the Comox Valley, and on visits to them, I became familiar with the Arts Alliance in Courtenay, which had a gallery, a meeting place for artists and musicians, and performance space. Budding from the Arts Alliance was the now legendary Renaissance Fair, where I performed for the first time during one of my visits to the Island.

In May of 1975, I met a handsome Swiss artist. Ben ended up moving in with me in September. We settled into domesticity, putting in a garden and buying two female goat kids, and enjoying the beauty of the bay. Just after New Year's in 1977, Doug contacted me. He had a new girlfriend and wanted to move back into the cabin. That had always been the agreement: he could have the cabin back when he wanted. It was fine with me, though I missed the rhythm of the tides and the stunning beauty of the bay terribly for months after leaving.

We decided to relocate to the Comox Valley. The music and arts, and our old friends, were a big draw for both of us. Arthur, a friend of ours who was renovating an empty house on Denman Island, said we could stay there while we looked for a house to rent. We didn't want to make our home on Denman Island, but it was a good place to be while we looked for a house to rent around Courtenay. We didn't have a vehicle, but Arthur had a school bus. He drove it to Oyster Bay, where he and Ben loaded all our possessions, our cat, our dog Lakshmi and our goats, Lavender and Rosemary. I made my own way from Vancouver once things were set up. While living in that partially renovated house, I began to feel quite ill. Everything smelled horrible. Foods I had enjoyed before now had no appeal. I lived on baked potatoes and butter and I hated salads. In the bath one morning I noticed that my breasts were different: sure enough, I was pregnant. Our move from Oyster Bay had been timely and fortuitous. There was no way I could have managed pregnancy and taking care of a baby at Oyster Bay. Having to be packed in and out was only one of the things that would have been almost impossible.

In April 1977, we found an old farmhouse to rent in Royston. Once again I performed at the summertime Renaissance Fair while Ben did set-up and sign painting. At the end of August we moved to another Royston house near the water three weeks before our daughter, Eliza, was born. The goats had a small pen and shed behind the house. They had not yet been bred and we would all go for walks along Marine Drive, the baby tied on to my chest, Lakshmi investigating all the smells on the way and the goats trotting along, eating bushes and weeds.

We wanted our own house and a place where we could garden and have some pasture for our goats. We found a small bungalow, again in Royston, this time near the village of Cumberland. We were able to purchase it with a down-payment loan from my parents and moved in on Halloween 1978. The house was on 2.9 acres of open and forested land with a seasonal creek and plenty of room for a garden, chickens, goats, ducks and, in time, a pony for Eliza.

We became part of the supportive community, and I continued to play music. I met Linda Safford at a food co-op meeting while I was living in

The contented new mom sitting in the September sunshine with baby Eliza and Laksh-mi, who's patiently waiting for her walk. Photo Ruben Kaufman

the house by the water. She and I became musical colleagues and friends and over the years have played at many venues, including cafés, fairs, farmers' markets and benefit concerts, and for several years we were part of a five-woman musical comedy revue troupe called the Fabulous Ms. Adventures, which toured on Vancouver Island and the Gulf Islands until 1999. We wrote and performed feminist political satire using skits and song. We still play together from time to time by request for special events.

I loved being a mother and longed for another baby, and in 1984 Belinda was born. Ben was a great dad during my pregnancies and when the children were small babies, but he seemed to lose interest once they became little people. His increasing binge drinking challenged our marriage. When the girls were four and eleven, Ben decided he could no longer handle family life and he left our home. For a couple of years he lived in Vancouver and

Courtenay, partially built a cabin at the far end of the property, remarried and then moved back to Switzerland for seven years. He became sober and now lives in the Interior of southern BC. His leaving was a blessing for me, but it was not easy for the girls to grow up without their dad.

For six years Eliza, Belinda and I were a tight unit. Life as a single parent was full, with all the business of running a household and driving kids to theatre classes, swim lessons, swim meets and tae kwon do lessons. I had given up the goats, chickens and ducks, as well as the garden. It was too much for me to handle on my own. Environmental concerns had become a priority in my life. I was arrested at the Kennedy Lake blockade in Clayoquot Sound in September of 1993. That weekend, I was with many other people from Courtenay and Hornby and Denman Islands. By then, over seven hundred people had already been arrested, and the process had become quite routine. I wanted a suspended sentence rather than house arrest, because I was a single parent. I did get one, but not for that reason: I was told it was because I was disabled. I was furious and felt patronized and demeaned.

In the autumn of 1993, I met Ross at the Bar None Café, a local meeting spot in the Comox Valley. He had also been arrested at Clayoquot Sound, but in 1992, in the early days when standing on the blockade was a truly brave act, in no way routine. At the time we met, he had cycled from the Robson Valley in search of a new home and was living at the Bevan hostel. At the café, he was asking if anyone knew of a spot where he could put in a garden. I offered up my neglected plots. One thing led to another and in the spring of 1994, Ross moved into my house. The children were not happy, but he weathered the storms and stuck it out. Eliza moved to Vancouver when she was eighteen to begin her adult life, and in 1996 Ross, Belinda and I travelled to India for three and a half months. Returning to my first home had been an unconscious desire during my childhood and a very conscious desire after my children were born. I'd been away for forty-three years. When the three of us travelled in India, we depended on each other, and Ross and Belinda bonded. Ross and I have been back to India twice since our first visit, also to Pakistan, and twice to Mexico. We travel well together.

The girls love Ross now and are both very close to him. This Halloween I will have been living in this house on "the land" for forty years. It's been through many changes: before Belinda was born, it was raised to include a foundation and full basement; a few years later, a bedroom was added; ten years ago a laundry room and a deck, where I grow flowers and herbs; and, recently, double-glazed windows. I still heat the house with a wood cook-stove and do my winter cooking on it, including Christmas dinners. I have never cooked a turkey in my electric oven. I'm still playing music, though not as much as before, and I'm still writing, not songs, now memoirs. In December 2016, after a twenty-three-year courtship, Ross and I secretly eloped to Vancouver and were quietly married by a marriage commissioner in Eliza's living room with both girls as witnesses. Seven months later we had a rollicking reception in our garden for family and friends. Our organic garden is huge and very productive. We are helped by young travellers who come to us through the WWOOF and HelpX programs. We have no goats, no chickens. Our neighbours have chickens and I can buy goat's milk at the supermarket. The system did not collapse as we were all preparing for, but the skills we learned in that preparation have served us well to this day.

Thirteen Houses

LINDA SAFFORD
Arrived in 1977

The seventies were a turbulent time in the world, and in my life. My long journey to the Comox Valley began in the late sixties with several significant events that radically changed my way of life: the Pentagon March, the Detroit Riots, moving to California and moving to Canada.

I was born in 1943, pre baby boom, and grew up in Detroit, Michigan, the youngest child of four in a working-class family. We lived in a two-storey house my parents bought just before I was born, and I was there all through my elementary, high school and early university years.

Dean was my high school sweetheart. Before grade 12 we stopped dating, and after high school graduation, we stayed friends but went our separate ways. Dean got married and had a son, Norman. I got a full-time job as a ward clerk at a hospital to save enough money to start university, eventually enrolling at Wayne State in the Department of Music. At the end of my first term, I went to the choir director to tell him how much I had enjoyed singing with him and that I hoped to be back for another semester after working to fund my further studies. He arranged a full-tuition music scholarship for me! I continued to work at a variety of part-time jobs, several in hospitals, to pay for living expenses and school texts and materials, while carrying a full-time course load. My parents contributed free room and board.

I graduated from Wayne State in April 1966 with a BA in music, and minors in sociology and psychology. Dean and his wife separated, and a mutual friend reconnected us. In May 1966, I travelled with Dean and three other friends from Detroit to Washington, DC, to a March Against the Vietnam War. An estimated eight thousand to ten thousand people took part. We stood facing soldiers who were holding rifles with attached bayonets. Later the soldiers dispersed the crowd with battering rams and tear gas; we fled in fear for our safety and our lives. When we returned to Detroit, we had a new under-standing of our relationship to and our alienation from the US government.

In September of 1966, I moved with Dean and Norman into a small, funky basement suite in the predominantly black ghetto bordering the university campus. In July 1967, we went camping for the weekend in Point Pelee Provincial Park, Ontario. While driving back to the US on a Monday morning, we heard bewildering news on the car radio about riots in Detroit. When we got to the Ambassador Bridge that connects Detroit with Windsor, we were stopped by police, as no one was allowed to enter the US. We went back to the campground for another night, listening to the news non-stop.

The next morning, when we drove back to the bridge, the officials said they were allowing only essential service workers into the US. When I said I was a social worker, they allowed us to enter. When we arrived in Detroit after that "Black Day in July," the only vehicles on the streets were police cars, each containing four officers wielding rifles pointed out the car windows, and tanks with armed soldiers seated on the turrets. When we got back to the apartment in the ghetto, there were bullet holes in the couch and the walls.

We moved out of that apartment, first into a high-rise downtown in a recently gentrified neighbourhood, and then into an old genteel mansion that we shared with several other friends. Just after Christmas in 1967, we decided to leave Detroit and move to San Francisco.

We arrived on New Year's Day, a little late for the Summer of Love. We stayed with friends until we found a three-room apartment on the cor-ner of Oak and Cole, on the panhandle of Golden Gate Park. The pan-handle was constantly active with outrageously, colourfully garbed people: teaching and practising tai chi, playing music, running, parents walking with children. We were in the heart of the Haight-Ashbury district. The traffic never stopped, day or night.

In November 1968, Matthew, our first child, was born. Very soon after, Beverly, Norman's birth mother, came and took Norman back to Detroit. I was devastated, having been his mother for just over a year. It was hard for me to adjust to being so far away from my family, my friends and my life in the world, with a new baby, and losing a child I loved.

I saw a poster for a women's liberation consciousness-raising session. I attended a meeting and became a part of an ongoing consciousness-raising group. Near our apartment, there was an urban commune called the Church of the Good Earth. One of the families within that commune became our closest friends during that period of our lives. The Good Earth sponsored a small communal farm, for people to learn and practise sustainable agriculture. They were also involved in urban social development activities, with a storefront office on Haight Street called Haight Ashbury Neighborhood Development (HAND). We visited the farm but we weren't yet ready to leave city life.

David, our second child, was born in May 1970 at home in our apartment on Cole Street. Dean's grandfather died and left him a significant amount of money. Dean bought a 1969 Volkswagen van, the kind with a pop-up top and a tent that opened out the back of the vehicle. It was like a small two-bedroom apartment. We took it to Baja, Mexico, for a short trip, and took our time coming home up the West Coast. En route we discovered some wonderful parkland and wilderness, something we two kids from Detroit had previously had little chance to explore. I had never considered where our drinking water came from, nor had I thought about where our solid waste went. Having two babies to care for slowed me down, and I looked around at the land that nurtured us and began to learn and understand our relationship to our earth. We spent a lot of time camping in Los Padres National Forest.

During this time, we met a lot of other folks with young families who were part of the back-to-the-land movement and became friends with two couples who had bought land in Humboldt County, with the intention of creating a working farm. They invited us to visit their homesteads, two forty-acre back-to-back parcels. They had built two houses about half a mile apart and were in the process of becoming self-sufficient and off the grid. When they had to leave their land to go back to the city for paid employment, they generously let us come and house-sit while they were away. I remember the gruelling 250-mile drive from San Francisco, arriving late in the day, getting the kids to sleep, building a fire, taking a few deep breaths and relaxing in the quiet atmosphere of a small hand-built house, away from the chaos and noise of the city. During this unsettled time, as we were travelling between the city and the bush, my mother died in Detroit.

In 1972 we decided to move to Humboldt County and live in the camper. We stayed on our friends' forty acres while we looked for land to buy. Dean and I were not getting along. When our friends left again, I moved into the Big House with the boys and Dean continued to live in the camper.

My dad loaned me the money to buy a Ford pickup truck with a 350 engine and a recycled chicken coop as a camper. A year later, he died.

We were incredibly lucky to live on this amazing homestead. Of all the places I lived in "the bush," this was by far the best. The ingenuity and talent that went into developing the systems that serviced the property were outstanding, and I learned a lot living there. The driveway (a dirt road about three-quarters of a mile long) was winding, ridged and rutted. It was a formidable task to keep the vehicle on the ridges and out of the ruts. I was always nervous when I had to drive that road! The Big House was at the top of a hill. Down the path from the house, a four-cylinder Crosley engine was installed in a spring, connected to a system that pumped water up to a holding tank on a hill above the house. To start the engine, it was necessary to touch two bare wires together. I was nervous about the pump, too; it had to be started about every third or fourth day, and I was scared every time.

The house was one and a half storeys high, heated by a wood stove made from a forty-gallon metal drum, which had been fitted with piping connected to a hot-water tank on the upper floor. The hot water was gravity fed to a bathtub and a kitchen sink on the floor below. There was no electricity; we used kerosene lamps and candles for lighting and propane for cooking.

There was a large, fenced garden area. I had never gardened before. I planted a whole package of pumpkin seeds, and voila! In a short time I had a *huge* crop of pumpkins. It was the beginning of my lifelong love for gardening.

I also helped to insulate the house by nailing tarpaper to the outside walls. I learned how to do simple vehicle repairs. I worked with a group of women who were operating a free school and helped to install rebar into the concrete on the building site.

When the owners came back, the boys and I moved into a tent on the property for the summer, and when the weather changed, we moved back to a communal house in San Francisco. While we were gone, Dean had an auto accident in Humboldt County and died. I had lost my mother, my father and my husband in the first three years of the seventies. I was in a brave new world, trying to raise two little boys.

After Dean's death, I considered moving back to Southern California to be near my sister, but I had become "bushed" and didn't want to live in a city. I spent a lot of time on the road, back and forth between Humboldt and another commune in Waldo, Oregon, where I met my friend Louise. I had written to our friends Sam and Ruth to let them know about Dean's death. They had made their way from San Francisco to Texada Island in BC and invited me to come and visit them there. I accepted their invitation and headed north from Oregon with the boys, Louise, her friend Robin, a fellow from Humboldt and our black Lab puppy.

Me and Dean by a campfire near the Big House in Humboldt County, California, 1972. Photo Paul Greenia

We were a travelling minstrel show: Robin was a dancer and three of us played guitar. We entertained a lot of people while waiting in ferry lineups. When we got to Texada, we met some local musicians at a weekly coffee house and spent a lot of time jamming. We camped on the beach and ate a lot of oysters. Sam earned his living picking salal and huckleberry.

Matty, me and David on Hornby Island, showing my brother, Ron, the sights of the Comox Valley, 1979. Photo by Ron Newcomb

Many of the people we met were tree planters and fishermen, occupations that had been completely unknown to me before I came to Canada.

Louise and Robin had both fallen in love with young men on Texada and decided to stay there, but the rest of us wanted to explore the Queen Charlotte Islands (now Haida Gwaii). On the Charlottes, people we met on Hippy Hill and elsewhere were friendly and helpful. We found a small (twelve-by-twelve-foot) plywood shack at Lawn Hill. It was a long hike, and we had to pack in all of our supplies, including plastic to cover bare spaces in the walls. We insulated the roof with moss and made a small wood stove out of a five-gallon can. We got our water from an open well, which we disinfected with chlorine bleach.

When Sam and Ruth decided to leave the Charlottes, I looked for a place to rent. The boys and I moved into a house in Skidegate Landing, owned by a family who had operated a nearby gas station. There had been a gas leak into the ground some years before, and the water in the house was contaminated. We had to pack bottled water in for drinking and washing. As soon as possible, I found another house to rent in the Village of Queen Charlotte.

There, a young single mom had started a daycare centre, operating out of the United Church. Her partner had a degree in urban planning and knew how to access funding. Dave Barrett was the new premier of BC and was implementing programs that served low-income people. We joined forces and got funding to build a building, with permission from the Skidegate Band to locate on their property. I was able to have my boys with me at work at the daycare. I looked after the children, managed the paperwork and drove the "bunny bus," a panel truck that picked up and dropped off the children.

Later, I was hired on a Local Initiatives Project grant to help rebuild the Charlotte City Community Hall, which had burned down. Then I was hired at the Charlotte City hospital, my work as a student in hospitals in Detroit serving me in good stead. I admitted and discharged patients, kept billing records, managed medical records, answered phones and typed correspondence.

Matt started kindergarten in Charlotte City and continued there through grade 2; David started kindergarten. One of the teachers took me under her wing, taught me how to manage a classroom and hired me as her substitute when she had to be away from school. The staff at the school encouraged me to go back to school to obtain a teaching certificate so that I could have summers off with my boys.

In August of 1976 I moved to Maillardville to attend Simon Fraser University. It was the first time I had lived in a city in many years. I rented a basement suite, sight unseen, by mail through the university housing office. It was another funky unit (shades of Detroit!), but it served us well for the year it took me to get my certificate.

In the spring of 1977, I was hired as a teacher by School District 71 in the Comox Valley. Anxious to get out of the city, I rented a cabin at the Alders in Merville, and once again we moved in August. It was a long drive from there to Airport School in Comox. The cabin wasn't insulated, and the only heat was an oil cookstove. We stayed there until January 1978, when we moved into a house on Condensory Road in Courtenay. In summer 1979, that house was sold and we had to move again. The housing situation then was dire; there were no places to rent. Fortunately I met a family who lived in Cumberland but were leaving for a year to attend university out of the country. We moved into their house in August (again). I spent the next year looking for a rental, but to no avail, so I began to look for a place to buy.

Just before they came back, I found a house. I was able to afford the down payment with money from an income tax refund and a matching loan from the wonderful teacher who had helped and encouraged me in the Charlottes. We moved into that house in August 1980, when Matt was twelve and David was ten. We had lived in thirteen houses before we finally found our family home.

And I am still living in that house!

Re-membering

ARDITH CHAMBERS
Arrived in 1978

A former, ephemeral self has developed a voice. She's pushing current me to re-member her by giving an account of my life from the late seventies on. She just doesn't realize how difficult it is to choose highlights, and besides, I am very busy.

"Busier than moving fifty-five milking cows from Duncan to Black Creek in one day between milkings?" she asks.

"Don't compare," I counter. Dairy farming was a hectic, demanding life-style with kids, husband, cows and other barnyard animals (rats included), but it was task driven, simply doing the next and the next chore, whereas today is a soft whorl of heart-centred activities that fully engages me.

In Duncan, we had started out as a three-person team (my husband, a teenage boy who was living with us, and me) milking cows and doing barn chores together. When ulcer attacks landed my husband in the hospital for a stretch, two of us carried the load. We were fortunate the teen was living with us at that critical time, as our two children were only three and eight years old. However, he didn't come along with us to Black Creek, so I became the milker, rising at 4 a.m. and out in the barn again at 3 p.m., not really minding the work because animals are lovely to be around. Hans was well enough to do all the other chores, but it was still difficult to get all the work done.

Farming went on for five years, and then we were off to a much easier life in a trailer home in Merville. I single parented while my husband went up north to construction jobs, and I did some teaching at Tsolum and Black Creek schools. I quite liked single parenting, but it didn't last long. My husband was excellent at setting up new business ventures; soon we were all together again as owners of a mom-and-pop grocery store in Cumberland, living quarters included. Life became hectic again with the store open for long hours, the kids needing preteen and teen guidance, and us schlepping

Clowning around with my granddaughter.

them to their various activities. I was again teaching part-time. Our marriage was slowly becoming un-glued, adding stress and draining time and energy. I felt a familiar loneliness when, after a year or so of store ownership, my husband was off to his next compelling interest. I carried on with the store, thankfully with the help of friends who worked for minimum wage.

The women working for us were more than nice to spend time with. I remember warm conversations when business was slow. Others that I met at the Courtenay Women's Centre gave me insight and energy. I felt validated and welcome, so I signed on for each upcoming group session even though, as an introvert, it was a struggle to reveal myself in the relaxed manner I saw others display. I wasn't aware of being part of the social change at that time, but I must have been, because I greatly admired and was influenced by women who were seeking a less traditional, more equal way of life. Asking for shared housework and meal making was a sign of my new-found confidence.

Over the next few years of upheaval, our family-owned store business ended, as well as our marriage. Our son moved out on his own, as did my husband. My daughter and I found temporary living quarters in Courtenay and then moved to Victoria for a year while I brushed up my teaching degree at the University of Victoria. I demanded an apology for being left to carry on without support and got it; then I found a way to forgive us both for our parts in the drama. The peace after forgiveness led to gratitude, years later, for all those experiences. I never would have started a business on my own, yet I had the joy of finding out that I could handle so much more than I originally thought, and now I fondly remember the good times.

"So, former self, is that enough, a good time to wrap it up?"

"No, it's still only the late eighties," bossy-she points out. "What about the absolute, really awful, complete breakdown you had after returning to Courtenay to teach, where you didn't even last the full year?"

"Oh, that year..." I was obsessed with a recurring vision of being on a raft in the middle of the ocean, no horizon in sight, an apt image for feeling adrift and purposeless. I understood how people could commit suicide, not that I planned to do it. Having my teenage daughter with me forced me to hold it together until I realized that I myself was the raft and I could even be the anchor to stop the drift. Slowly a light formed on the horizon as we made future plans, my daughter to Switzerland as an exchange student, me to New Westminster to live with my brother and his family until I got my feet on the ground.

The temporary stay at my brother's lasted fourteen years, and I lived in the attic of their huge heritage house. I had a grand time learning restoration techniques and sharing the satisfaction of salvaging the original after it had been a care home for decades. I worked part-time in two libraries, Burnaby Public and Douglas College. I loved the city, I loved my work; living in the attic of a heritage house was straight out of a movie. Romance even hovered for a couple of years until I recognized I was setting myself up again to maintain someone else's ideas and lifestyle. What needed firming up was a mystery for quite a while, but then resolve came when I joined a peer-counselling group where active listening was highly praised. With practice, pure listening became an act of generosity from me, and I found it very satisfying for both the listener and the speaker. No need to commit myself full-time and help fulfill another's dream in order to have a fulfilling connection.

After years of bliss, my brother's wife, originally from Texas, pined for her home country, so they moved across the border to Blaine, Washington. Restoration work halted and renters moved in, swiftly changing the dynamics of living there. A visiting lacrosse team bunking in the rooms for a summer meant very little quiet or sleep in my attic. Then, when one renter dipped into insanity, terrorizing the rest of us until the police were called, I decided to act on my daughter and son-in-law's offer for me to move back to Courtenay to live with them (toddler included).

Less bossy now, my former self suggests I write about fifteen years of living in the Comox Valley again. Advancing age means fewer physical activities, but I love being able to do what I please: previewing for the World Community Film Fest; fundraising for African grannies; giving Healing

How I celebrated my seventy-fifth birthday.

Touch therapy; and companioning people in their last stage of life through hospice work. It suits me to go from a large attic to a tiny basement suite and share a house, a car and big decisions that affect us all.

The four of us respect each other's privacy and have learned to give lots of leeway for personality foibles. I keep a connection with the teen who had lived with us years ago, as well as his family; he cooks a great Sunday supper that acts like a party.

My granddaughter and I have outgrown jumping on the trampoline and dressing like clowns; now I proudly buy tickets to watch her sing in musical theatre productions. I get my city fix two or three times a year, often looking after former library co-workers' pets when they go away, or staying with my son and his wife in their Surrey home, which aspires to be as huge as the big old heritage.

In my half-formed state in the seventies, I never had a vision of what life should be like. I didn't question what came my way. I dealt with issues by throwing my shoulder to the wheel. As a young person, I believed that I could handle anything. Life proved me wrong, but in hindsight, I see more upsides than downsides to the overwhelming situations that seemed so difficult while I was stewing in them. Now I say thanks for the experiences that created a more defined and appreciative person. My hardships were nothing compared to those of most of the world's population. Coming full circle, I see value in accepting life without question, but this time from the opposite side of innocence. I am confident everything will turn out fine. It always has.

My Island Story

LINDA DENEER
Arrived in 1978

The back wall of the vintage trailer, behind our makeshift bed, was covered by a glistening crop of mysterious-looking mushrooms. I had decided that it was time to do a serious spring cleaning of the old trailer we had spent the last winter in and had pulled the bed away from the wall. Upon seeing these alien life forms happily growing there, my first thought was to hurry home to my mother. The trailer roof had been leaking over the winter. My husband had covered the roof with a large blue tarp. The excessive condensation inside had promoted the unwanted fungal growth.

We had moved this trailer, which on the inside resembled an old European train car, onto the property we had purchased in Black Creek. We had no electricity for the first year, as we had no extra money available to purchase a pole and the trailer would not pass an electrical inspection. That was one of many challenges we faced living in the eight-by-twenty-eight-foot 1940ish vintage trailer. We kept perishable food in a bucket, which we lowered by rope down into the well to keep it cool. An A-frame outhouse was built nearby, kerosene lanterns were used for light and an ancient oil stove gave us heat. Our infant slept in a tiny playpen at the end of our bed, next to the outside door, and our other boy slept in an alcove in a hallway. The trailer would settle with the fluctuating freezes and thaws, popping the back door wide open in the night.

Despite these conditions, both children remained happy and healthy during this time. Our family would drive to the local swimming pool several times a week to avail ourselves of the showers. Cloth diapers were rinsed in buckets and taken to the laundromat, as we had no running water. The trips in our old car to town were at times quite interesting. My uncle had sold us his old Chevrolet Impala while we lived in Alberta. After a few months of

Enjoying tea with the family on our deck.

island humidity, the car began to develop some interesting quirks. The back doors ceased to close properly, and when we were rounding a corner, a back door would swing wide open. We solved that dilemma by using ropes to attach the inside handles, one to the other, to keep the doors closed.

I worked twelve-hour shifts as a nurse at the Campbell River Hospital while my husband cared for our children and slowly built our house. Hans had worked in foreign exchange for a large bank in Rotterdam, the Netherlands. He had no experience in construction or a rural lifestyle. He received guidance from dear elderly friends who mentored him on how to build a house, a slow and often agonizing process for three years, as we had no mortgage and paid for materials paycheque to paycheque. Hans found work as a machinery painter and in construction. We gradually cleared trees and planted a vegetable garden and fruit trees. We moved into a largely unfinished house. What a joy it was to see the well-worn, dilapidated trailer get towed off the property to another property in the vicinity! During this time of building and scraping out a homestead, we enjoyed a rollicking social life with like-minded neighbours who were doing the same. Many of our neighbours lived in rustic cabins and geodesic domes. We enjoyed bringing home hitchhikers, and going to dances, potluck dinners and other events at friends' homes and at the Black Creek Hall. Summer brought the Renaissance Fair, a highlight.

On our way to the Island.

Our path to Black Creek had been circuitous. Years before, my sister Judy and I had set out from Alberta for Asia to work as nurses at a missionary hospital in the mountains of Taiwan. We flew to Singapore and came up with the idea of first exploring Southeast Asia before taking up the nursing positions. This was the start of an adventure that changed both our lives. It was exhilarating for two young women to travel that part of the world in the early seventies; we would look at a map and decide that a certain country looked interesting, and off we would journey to see it. Months into this adventure, after trekking on the glorious Annapurna trail in Nepal, we met two lads from the Netherlands. We began travelling together, stopping for several months in Australia and New Zealand to earn money to continue our travels. Judy and I decided against going to Taiwan to work but chose to continue the carefree nomadic life in exotic locales with our Dutchmen. After extensive travels and many unforgettable experiences, the four of us arrived in the Netherlands, where Judy and I worked as nurses and I gave birth to our first-born.

When I felt I needed to introduce our baby to my family, Hans and I, with the baby, went off to Canada to my parents' farm in Southern Alberta, where we lived for a year. While in Alberta, my school friend Sally had

Scraping through rocks to plant our first garden.

visited us at the farm and urged us to come visit her and check out Vancouver Island. The Alberta winter had been long and brutal, so we decided to take her up on the invitation. In the spring, we hit the road in a homemade camper, headed for the Island.

Crawling out of our camper on a glorious March day in 1978, we found ourselves on a new path in life. The evening before, we had driven up Island in the dense dark and driving rain to visit another old friend and her partner in Black Creek. Because we had never been to the Island before, we had no idea how to find the home of our friend, so we sought a place to park our camper for the night. We veered off the Island Highway and ended up in a parking lot. Exhausted, the three of us crawled into the back of the camper. We awoke to brilliant blue skies, eagles calling, towering Douglas firs, spring vegetation, glorious mountain vistas and a view of the snow-capped mountains on the mainland. We discovered we were at Miracle Beach Provincial Park. What a joyous introduction it was to the Island! My husband and I had spent time in New Zealand, Australia and Southeast Asia, where we first met, and had often spoken dreamily during those carefree travelling days of settling down in a little house in the BC wilderness. That morning at the Miracle Beach parking lot, we felt that we had truly found the ideal home of our earlier fantasies.

Although our lives were busy, there was time to enjoy the beauty of the Island and develop the close bonds with friends and neighbours that continue to this day. People came here from all over Canada and other parts of the world, drawn like we were to the natural splendour and freedom. There were tenting trips, interesting people and festivals. There was good music. The beauty and friendliness of the Comox Valley and Campbell River were inspiring. Hans and I felt we had arrived at our true home the moment we walked down the pathway to the ocean at Miracle Beach Park that spring morning. That feeling has only strengthened in the years since. We have stayed at the same location. It amazes me that we now enjoy a comfortable home, mature gardens and a network of family and friends that sustain us. The beauty of the Island and the Comox Valley continues to astound me and fill me with gratitude.

Quest for Community

JOSEPHINE PEYTON
Arrived in 1978

As a child, I always longed for family. I'm not talking about a nuclear family, for I had a mother, a father, two brothers and a sister. I'm talking about the extended family most children grow up knowing: grandparents, cousins, aunts, uncles and even close friends of parents. My earliest dreams were about belonging, but I was always the outsider. I think I was always looking for community.

My teenage years were spent in the numbingly conservative outskirts of Vancouver, in a newly built suburban community called Ranch Park in Coquitlam. I didn't know the neighbours beyond a friendly hello or a babysitting job. Before I left home, my parents had occasionally provided a roof to young American draft dodgers while they sorted out their next move. However, I was largely unaffected by the world around me.

In 1968, at the age of eighteen, my world quickly grew much larger. I found myself in San Francisco for the summer, a guest of my older brother, who lived in a large communal house of more than forty people dedicated to change and focussed on social justice and gestalt therapy. The therapy I experimented with was practised in large groups paying for weekend-bingeing, fast-tracked awareness for those seeking to heal family-of-origin wounds. We were Age of Aquarius people. Sleep deprivation, alter-ego soothsayers, sensory music and a psychologist helped us unravel emotional scars with surprising sweetness. Heart pounding, I was screaming my way awake, to the songs from the musical *Hair* played at a deafening volume and the realization that I had been living my parents' dream, not mine. Almost instantly I was, or at least felt, transformed. I had arrived on the doorstep of the tune-in/drop out hippie counterculture.

There is a safe way to be awakened: hook up with another like-minded soul. In my case it was Ernie Yacub, who had a compelling story of his own and who was already making a name for himself in the arena of environmental activism and community development. Our mutual yearning for community and for making a profound change in the way people live together was our common bond. In 1972 we quit our jobs, got together with a small group of like-minded people, applied for grants and spent thousands of hours embroiled in the nitty-gritty work of putting some of these ideas into physical form, designing and fabricating a community that we eventually called Community Alternatives. We gave a lot of attention to guiding principles and codes for living together, as well as complicated methods of conflict resolution. There were endless details to attend to. Not everyone was satisfied with city living, and we had a genuine desire to be self-sustaining. The design evolved to include a rural component, now called Fraser Common Farm. This integrated rural-urban community is quite unique and still thriving in Vancouver and Aldergrove.

I was restless. Almost three years into the design process, I grew tired of the very people I was planning to spend my life and labour with. The fit wasn't right. Older, conservative, well-educated people with down-to-earth dreams didn't match the edgy, radical (left-leaning) politics of my idealistic, relatively carefree twenties. Also, I was anxious to continue deeper into my personal journey. Concepts articulated on chalkboard and thrashed around in endless meetings did not feed my desire to raise children, dig in the soil and grow food for the table. My biological clock was ticking.

Ernie and I toured the province in search of a new home. We talked to some rural-based intentional communities and found that they almost universally struggled. Money was a divisive issue. Intentional communities needed to be financially solvent, but the dichotomy between the people who earned money outside the community and the people who laboured within it created tension. I was beginning to understand the concept of right livelihood and its significance for the survival of the back-to-the-land movement that was blossoming in BC in the seventies.

Right livelihood or "do no harm" comes from the teaching of the Buddha. I was reading the *Whole Earth Catalogue* and the *Foxfire* books to understand the importance of ethical work as a service, to myself and for the welfare of the planet. We were dreaming of a better way to coexist.

Along the road that winter, we stumbled into a small intentional community in Lumby called An Alternate Community. It was a turning point for us. This raggle-taggle group of enterprising people talked and partied with us over several nights. Around the pink-insulation-festooned walls of a partially built shack, they too, in the context of their community process, had come to the same conclusion around right livelihood. We discussed lots of possibilities; tree planting was eventually chosen. In 1976 nine of us ventured forth on our first tree-planting contract with only one slightly experienced planter, all of us crammed into and onto a Volkswagen Beetle with an assortment of various worn tools. Skookum Reforestation Cooperative Association was born. To us, Skookum, a word in use by coastal First Nations, meant "better than all right," "solid and real," "cool" and "dependable." It seemed to encapsulate our collective ideals.

In the mid-seventies, Skookum Reforestation was the province's only non-profit silviculture enterprise. We used a consensus model, hired women, guaranteed equal and fair pay, offered full benefits, had unparalleled safety practices and worked reasonable hours in a competitive arena in an era when seasonal work was largely unregulated. There were the inevitable meetings, grievances were aired in "clearing sessions," and we addressed issues in a feminist context, briefly forming a women's collective within the co-op. Everyone contributed to the 10 percent fund that was disbursed annually to support other non-profits and altruistic endeavours, and to fund a few three-day gatherings that were a mixture of a little business and a lot of partying, the building blocks of bonding.

By spring 1978, tree planting was in full swing. Our average crew size was fifteen and, notably, half came from Merville in the Comox Valley. We were thriving in spite of our unorthodox approach and we were gelling as a close-knit community of workers. Skookum was a lifestyle, somewhat nomadic, earthy and tribal. I made good friends. I had a real sense of belonging. I loved the rawness of the work. However, I was three months pregnant and still homeless. Gary, a tree planter and one of the original members of An Alternate Community, was convinced he knew the perfect spot for us. I remember his words well: "Cumberland is the town for you, and not only is it the perfect town, you should live on Camp Road. You will fit right in and be happy there." How right he was.

When Ernie and I came to the valley in 1978, we immediately fell in love with Cumberland. It was a working-class town with strong union roots and families who had been there for generations. Newcomers, as we were called, were helping the town survive. The coal mines had closed years earlier and families were hanging on, but local jobs were scarce, and most wage earners worked away in logging camps along the coast or in mines in northern BC. As recommended, we found a house on Camp Road and

Outfitted with thrift-store finds and wearing rubber caulk boots, I was geared for tree planting. Photo Ernie Yacub

immediately knew it was the spot for us. We were not alone. Other young people were discovering the crumbling charm of the largely forgotten town amid the bustle of the more economically viable Comox Valley. A cynical person might have said Cumberland was just a place to get in the market, but the young families that came in the seventies didn't move away. Cumberland was affordable, but it also offered something more intangible. It behaved like a real community. We didn't need to fit in, because nobody seemed to care about the fit. Cumberland has a proud history of taking care of its own. The Campbell Brothers General Store had extended credit to striking miners' families between 1912 and 1914, and to this day residents rally around families hit with hard times. Whether they are newcomers or have been here for generations, Cumberlanders are fiercely loyal to their community.

The dust of moving had not yet settled when a neighbour I met at the local chapter of the Merville organic food-buying co-op offered to help me get ready for my home birth. I was overdue and anxious that the little house we had moved into needed a thorough clean. Three months pregnant

My garden was a source of healthy food for the family. It was also my respite from a noisy household. Photo Ernie Yacub

with her first child, Lee Bjarnason, another newcomer to Cumberland, scrubbed and waxed the old linoleum floor, circa the fifties, on her hands and knees. Similar acts of kindness and service have been Lee's legacy here. Lee and Jeanine Maars started a preschool called Small World Nursery School at the Masonic Hall, and a decade later Lee and I became work buddies at the Comox Valley Child Development Association.

It didn't take long to meet my neighbours. Camp Road is quaint and aged, with houses set close to the road. From front porches, the activity on the road is visible and interesting. With a nothing-to-lose attitude, Cumberland folks would belt out a hearty hello and comments about the weather. Rural people are curious but also looking for connection. It was likely that we would see each other again at the bank, post office or at Leung's, the only grocery store in town, and continue the conversation.

In 1978 there were six tree-planting families on the block, representing six different companies. There were at least six young mothers with one or two children each, and we all knew each other. I have delightful, rich memories of walking with my daughter "down Camp," and by the end of the road there would be a collection of women with children walking together. The destination was not as important as the conversation, typically worries about child rearing, in endless microscopic detail. When our children were old enough, they walked along the road to pop into their friends' homes and they were always welcomed. Those were good times.

As the seventies ended, I was thoroughly ensconced with raising children, growing food and running a business. Somehow, though, there was always time for a good party. On another block in town, a neighbour always hosted an annual potluck Women's Day brunch on the Sunday closest to March 8. We would leave our children at home, bring our best dishes and gleefully celebrate our uninterrupted conversations. Gloria Simpson, a neighbour down Camp, hosted an Empire Days barbecue

My life in Cumberland was centred around family and community. My adult children still have deep roots here. Photo Ernie Yacub

every May. In her multi-tiered garden, children would run amok without repercussions, as long as they took care of each other. Our Merville kin hosted many parties year-round, always with astoundingly good live music late into the night. Children, like the dogs, would just drop asleep on floors and couches, exhausted but completely happy to be included in the reverie.

Almost four decades later, I am in the same spot. I have a son who has bought a house six doors down and a daughter who has come home to have her first child. I have built roots in this community. I imagine I will die here. Cumberland's character is in its history, its untidiness and frayed but sturdy seams. Like a well-worn cloak, it has embraced me and kept me warm. We keep our community's attributes under that cloak, not wanting our perfect spot, our little piece of nirvana, to be discovered by developers or others who may not appreciate what we have here. Becoming a mother here was the most profound and rewarding event of my life. I will always be grateful to the women of this rural community for supporting me and becoming my tribe. I didn't have to invent and design my community. It was here waiting for me to discover it.

Home Is Where the Heart Is

GWYN SPROULE
Arrived in 1978

It was love that brought me to the Comox Valley. I came because of Jamie Sproule. Looking back, it is a kind of miracle that we met at all. So many things were against it, not the least of which being the fact that I was in England and he was in the Comox Valley. I'd travelled to Western Canada the year before and returned home to Sheffield. I had no real plans to return; I was resigned to making a life in Margaret Thatcher's England. Then a close friend reminded me that I'd promised to take her to BC. A promise is a promise, so the spring of 1978 found us living as cheaply as possible in a tiny cabin on Jawbone Creek near Likely in the Cariboo Mountains. I knew the area well from my earlier trip, and it didn't take us long to get into the rhythm of life in Likely.

Friday was mail day, and all the cabin dwellers came into town for supplies and to get together with friends at the Likely Hotel. One particular Friday afternoon, just after I arrived, a phone call came for me on the house phone. It was a tree-planting contractor, Claude of Greenwood Family Rainbow Cooperative, offering me a tree-planting job near 100 Mile House. The first person I met when I arrived at the camp was the cook, Jamie. He was friendly and cheerful, a generous cook who made all his own bread, yogurt and baked goods, as well as wholesome vegetarian food. At the end of the job, everyone was heading off in different directions. Jamie invited my friend June and me to visit him in Cumberland if we ever came that way. He said he had a house in Cumberland and a barge in the Courtenay Slough. He also told us about the Renaissance Fair in early July. My friend and I went down for that weekend and stayed with Jamie at his cabin on Comox Lake Road, along with other friends from the tree-planting camp.

At the end of the weekend, as I was leaving to go back to Likely, Jamie asked me if I would come back again. I said yes, but in my heart I wasn't sure. I returned to my cabin for two weeks. I couldn't stop thinking about Jamie, how kind and funny he was and how he wanted me to come back. I packed up everything I owned and headed back to the Island, travelling on the CPR night ferry from downtown Vancouver to Nanaimo. I arrived back in Cumberland early on a Sunday morning. As I approached Jamie's little house on Comox Lake Road, I saw a clean-shaven face looking out of the front window. I didn't recognize him at first, but it was Jamie, and he'd shaved off his beard. He was no longer wearing his high school horn-rimmed glasses fastened around his head with elastic bands. His long hair was brushed out. He was radiant. Later, he told me that he had been looking out the window every day for two weeks, knowing I would be coming back.

I said that I was staying for only a few days before going on to Tofino to find work on a fishboat. Jamie suggested I stay a bit longer. I never left. Jamie's cabin was very rustic. The tall grass grew right to the front door. There were four other houses, and ours was the last in the row. Originally, there had been about thirty houses in this neighbourhood when African-American miners (most were freed slaves, all now gone) lived here. Over the road was the site of the No. 1 Japanese Town, and in the other direction was Chinatown, once the second-largest Chinatown on the west coast of North America. The latter had been razed to the ground in 1968, just ten years before I came to live in the neighbourhood. I felt a great sense of loss, even though I had very little knowledge of local history at that time. Everywhere I walked around the site, there were bits of pottery and other artifacts. I could almost feel Chinatown as it had been.

One really hot day, we decided to drive up to Forbidden Plateau in Jamie's old convertible Morris Minor. Predictably, it overheated about halfway up the steep switchbacks of the road to the ski hill. We abandoned the car and carried on walking uphill. Just before we collapsed from heat exhaustion, we rounded a corner and there was a huge green wooden building with the sign Forbidden Plateau Lodge and a smaller sign saying Bar. We could scarcely believe our eyes. In the bar, over a cold cider, we got talking to the manager, Vince. As it happened, they needed a cook and a housekeeper for the ski season. Jamie and I applied for the jobs, and in late 1978 we moved to the lodge. Our lives became intertwined with Forbidden Plateau.

The lodge dated back to the early thirties, when a local entrepreneur had operated a business, bringing tourists from all over the world to stay and outfitting them with mules, guides and supplies. They would ride up the

Mount Becher Trail and over to the Dove Creek Trail and then back to the lodge. Forbidden Plateau Lodge had continued to operate as a guest house since that time. Now it catered to skiers in the winter season and offered a small outdoor summer program.

In the winter, we often had between fifty and a hundred guests on a weekend. On Friday night we always served spaghetti bolognese, and on Saturday it was turkey. Local groups such as the Mountaineering Club and Skookum Reforestation would have their Christmas parties at the lodge. The same families came every year for reunions. Some of our friends got married there. In 1980 Jamie and I were married there as well; it was a grand affair. In winter, the ski hill workers would stop by the bar after work. We sometimes held dances with live music from our house band, the Real Live Dance Band. The parties lasted the whole weekend.

During the summers of 1978 and 1979, Jamie and I lived on our barge at the Courtenay Slough. One summer we got a tow behind Claude's wooden sailboat, the *Daemon*, to Ford's Cove on Hornby Island. We tied up to the dock there and did repairs over the course of two months. At the end of the summer, we got a tow back to Courtenay Slough.

Every spring, we went tree planting in the Cariboo, returning to the lodge in time to run our summer program. We offered outdoor education programs to School District 71 and took children hiking, camping, canoeing and rock climbing in order to build their self-confidence.

The year 1981 was a big one. Most significantly, our daughter Flora was born that spring. In the summer, the lodge hosted the Comox Valley Women's Festival. The weather was perfect, and most of the workshops took place outside. I taught two courses, one on making wines and another on wild edible plants.

In the fall, we would usually travel to see our families in England and Ottawa. Then would come winter, and the lodge would be brimming with mirth and merriment. Guests came back from skiing at the end of the day in great spirits. The German families living in neighbouring cabins would come to the lodge some evenings to play table tennis. It was truly a memorable time in our lives: we worked, we skied and we met lots of wonderful people. We were part of the fabric of the ski hill. We thought we would live like that forever.

In the spring of 1982, Jamie and I got a cooking contract at a tree-planting camp up near Smithers. We loaded up the Volvo and travelled to Prince Rupert by ferry and to Smithers by road. We were able to work as cooks as well as look after Flora, who was then almost one year old.

At the camp, Jamie built a fine plastic shack for us to live in, with a stove and chimney. It was cozy and bright. Two months went by; then it was time to return to the lodge to run our summer programs. We set off on the long journey back to the Island by road. After two long days of travel, we reached Courtenay and picked up a young friend of ours who was hitchhiking. He gave us news that would change our lives, although at first we didn't believe him. He told us the lodge had burned down the previous day. We

Taken on my wedding day at Forbidden Plateau Lodge, August 23, 1980. Photo John Clark

didn't truly accept it until we met Vince, our partner, who confirmed the terrible news. The next day we went to look at the charred ruins. There was nothing left. The building was made of tinder-dry cedar and had gone straight up in flames in a very short time. We lost everything: our clothes, skis, wedding gifts and livelihood.

We moved to Bevan Lodge for the summer and ran our outdoor program from there, including another Women's Festival. Then we found a small cabin on Forbidden Plateau Road where we could stay for the winter. We continued to ski at Forbidden that winter, trying not to think about where we would live when spring came around.

One Sunday, our friends Rick and Yvonne drove over from Cumberland to tell us that the Green House, Jamie's old cabin, was empty again. When we phoned the owner and asked if we could rent it, she said she planned to leave it empty and sell it in the summer. We immediately made a very low offer on the house, which she refused, but our second offer was accepted, and we moved in that spring. The house was very basic. It was a miner's cabin that had been built in 1888, and it had a small lean-to on the back. It seemed hardly big enough to raise a family. The yard was somewhat neglected, but it was almost buried in white snowdrops and purple violets that March. I fell in love with it all. Our daughter Annabelle was born in the house at Christmas that year. Even though home births were not permitted at that time, we had

Jamie and me at the Green House with baby Annabelle, three-year-old Flora and family dog Megan. Spring 1984.

two experienced midwives with us, and Annabelle was a healthy baby. We had a very quiet Christmas, just the four of us, in that tiny house. It was minus twelve Celsius outside, and there was no insulation in the walls, but we had two wood stoves cranking continuously, so we were cozy. Soon we had a small farm happening, with goats, chickens, ducks and rabbits. I learned to be an efficient goat milker and made yogurt and cheese with the milk. For the next few years, we lived a pretty idyllic West Coast life. We continued to plant trees, working and playing in the outdoors, raising our girls and making improvements to the Green House. Our family became deeply rooted in the Cumberland community, with Jamie and

Jamie, Flora and me on Mount Becher. Spring 1982.

I eventually working in the local schools. My passion for the environment and for the history of the place led me to stand successfully for Cumberland council.

In 1998 came more life-changing news. Jamie was diagnosed with early-onset Parkinson's. He was only forty-seven.

Life carried on, but with a realization of how precious time was. While Jamie's health permitted, we continued to enjoy the outdoors, and we took as many trips as we could around the world, visiting Peru, Cuba, Mexico, Greece and New Zealand. Inevitably, Jamie's condition worsened and he passed away in January 2018 at the age of sixty-eight.

Our girls and their families have settled in the Comox Valley. Home is where the heart is, and mine is firmly placed here. I still live in the Green

House and am still a Cumberland village councillor. Our family loves this place, for its beauty, the community and our rich store of memories. As I was watching my grandchildren play in the historic orchard only yesterday, I thought for the umpteenth time how very lucky it was that chance brought Jamie and me together.

Beneath the Glacier in Blue

LYNDA GLOVER
Arrived in 1979

I love the lyrics of the song "Blue" by Joni Mitchell, which was released in 1970. My favourite colour, blue, has always been a theme in my life. Growing up as an only child in East Vancouver, I spent hours using my imagination. Sweet memories of childhood include singing old songs as we washed dishes and learning about blue flowers in our garden. Mom encouraged me to draw and paint; Dad taught me how to jive to "Blue Suede Shoes" by Elvis. I grew up singing, dancing, gardening, drawing and painting.

On a European trip, a friend and I arrived in Amsterdam to discover the opening of the Vincent Van Gogh Museum. Seeing *The Starry Night* and *Wheatfield with Crows*, I thought of Van Gogh's words: "To understand blue you must first understand yellow and orange." Anne and I travelled through Europe, devouring galleries and countrysides. I planned paintings.

The same year that I travelled to Europe, I met Ross, a blue-eyed man with a blue plaid shirt, faded blue jeans and a blue Volkswagen Bug. In 1978 close friends and family gathered in Horseshoe Bay at the Gleneagles Golf Course in front of a roaring fireplace while we became Mr. and Mrs. Glover. My friend Anne returned from Algiers and wore the blue dress I had sewn to wear as her maid of honour the December before. We shared a memorable day of love, music and dancing.

Ross had worked out of town in Canada and other countries (the Northwest Territories, Peru, Paraguay and Iran) for more time than he was home. A job was offered in Borneo, and I dreamed of joining him to study natural dyes. Indigo symbolized magic, wisdom and spirit in history. I was eager to experience the colour, smell and endless possibilities of creating blue tones. I would stitch and tie natural fabrics tightly, then soak the tied fabric, weighted with stones, in the rich crusty dye. Soon we learned he would share a tent in the jungle with bugs and reptiles, not me!

My first Comox Valley salmon, caught on my dad's Peetz fishing reel.

Our lives changed. Ross became the manager of surveying for McElhanney in Courtenay, a chance to work closer to home. We announced to friends that we were going "overseas" to Vancouver Island. In March Ross moved to Courtenay, close to the railway tracks and the ocean, to start work. I continued working at Gleneagles Elementary School in Horseshoe Bay, teaching and coordinating art for the district. I visited Ross on weekends. In May I organized an art workshop for teachers in the Comox Valley. At the elementary school in Comox, many teachers participated in my hands-on workshop. An interview followed, and I was hired as the part-time art coordinator for grades K through 12, starting in September. I was the only female coordinator in the district at the time, and I shared office space with five to eight men.

First, though, came a magical summer. We trolled for coho salmon through boils of herring off the far shores of Tree Island using a lucky lure from my dad's tackle box. We grilled wild asparagus and silver-scaled salmon on our small hibachi and served them with delicately fluted oysters picked near Flora Islet in Helliwell Provincial Park. The hibachi was one of the few possessions that we fit into the tiny suite of an Austrian home on Holiday Road in Fanny Bay. I adored taking trips to Denman and Hornby Islands during the days while Ross worked. I began filling my camera with irresistible images, collecting moon-snail shells for continuous line drawings and taking rubbings on sandstone rocks of First Nation petroglyphs. Searching for blue landscapes by bicycle became my favourite pastime that summer. Apparently life was a holiday on Holiday Road.

I met up with my childhood friend Linda Rajotte, who was teaching in the valley. We had always loved to sing, dance and play together. Our rendition of "Lavender's Blue (Dilly Dilly)" had kept our parents in stitches. I was excited to be near her and share artistic pursuits. Van Gogh said, "Colour in painting is like enthusiasm in life." My enthusiasm for the Comox Valley life was just beginning. My palette was waiting, with so many new images to paint.

Ross's job as a surveyor was to measure, map and draw up property lines. Most weekends were filled with wilderness adventures in Strathcona Provincial Park, exploring Mount Washington, Paradise Meadows and the surrounding areas. While Ross envisioned the new ski hill, the moss-covered rocky crags and forests taught me about texture and depth, with so many greens to discover. The meadows showed movement and light, reminding me of Emily Carr paintings where one could dance to the music of her brush strokes. Canoe trips on Comox, Tsable, Willemar and Forbush Lakes helped me memorize colours and patterns of reflections and light. While snowshoeing on Forbidden Plateau, I captured photos of sparkling sun and shadows on snow. Beachcombing provided time to search for treasure. I watched crows, ravens and eagles to capture their form and movement and to relate to their personalities and habits. Experiencing and painting nature brought me pleasure and joy. We made weekend trips to Vancouver, but as soon as we were back on the Old Island Highway, it felt like we were coming home.

In September my job as art coordinator took me to schools from Hornby Island and Union Bay to Miracle Beach. My students eagerly helped the Travelling Art Lady haul totes laden with art materials to classrooms. Each week I conducted art workshops and demonstration lessons for teachers. I created lessons based on various art techniques and local themes. We painted trumpeter swans, collaged spawning salmon and drew pastel eagles with resist washes of watercolour. Seasonal themes based on music, language arts, science and social studies became art units to provide teachers with booklets so they could confidently return to classrooms and teach art. Today, I still see those art ideas displayed in hallways. That fall I also offered a series of natural-dye workshops through the North Island College. Classes filled in September with a new circle of friends eager to dip their hands into blue dyes. Creating with indigo became my passport to friendships. Invitations to campgrounds, dinners, parties and dances followed.

Drawing blue sea life on Cathie's hand-thrown porcelain led to participating in pottery shows, joining the Potters' and Weavers' guilds, and helping found the original Potters Place Store. Each experience introduced me to artists who loved to draw and paint outdoors. We created batiks, dyed with indigo and framed large hangings to decorate the blue lounge walls of the Forbidden Plateau Lodge. The original Renaissance Fair attracted us not only for the art, but also for the music. For many years Cathie and I set up our booth there with pottery, fabrics and paintings, and we continued to do so at the Filberg Festival.

Our Comox Valley lives were filled with work and sports: skiing, golf, hockey, curling, football, tennis, squash and baseball. In December 1979, we moved to our first home in Comox, threw out the purple shag rugs, decorated with furniture recovered in blue, painted walls and repurposed second-hand bricks, blue boards, crates and tiles to make our house a home. We built our first greenhouse, stretching plastic sheeting over a wood frame. Inside, rich black soil filled the raised beds, covered with seaweed left behind in piles on the beach by winter storms. Soon we harvested organic greens, plump tomatoes and vegetables to add to our diet of local seafood. Our family grew when our son Jon was born in 1981, followed by another son, Pat, in 1983. As Lawren Harris said, "We lived in a continuous blaze of enthusiasm....Above all we loved this country and loved exploring and painting it!" Our busy family loved everything about the Comox Valley and I couldn't wait to start painting it! Since then, I have painted spawning salmon, crows, ravens, eagles, flowers, lakes, trees and meadows.

For twenty-five years, we've lived in Croteau Beach on the Comox Harbour. We joined with neighbours to save MacDonald Wood and have been challenged by the possibility of a large sewage pump station near our backyard. Our yard has a forest, a greenhouse, a fenced garden and an orchard of apple, plum, pear and nut trees. While working in my vegetable garden or weeding potted flowers on the deck, I'm studying poppies, sunflowers and hydrangeas to add to a canvas later. Ross is steward to the tree (the "Eagle Tree") where our two eagles, Gertrude and Heathcliff, preside over our two acres. We wake up to look at the Comox Glacier when morning sunrises bathe the peaks. I think of the Queneesh stories, its historical importance and the symbol it has become for the Comox Valley. As climate change causes the Comox Glacier to recede, I wonder if our symbol of the valley will be lost for future generations.

Georgia O'Keeffe wrote about the importance of the Cerro Pedernal, a narrow mesa mountain in northern New Mexico. She saw it from the Ghost Ranch each morning and evening and decided to paint it one hundred times in different lights, times of day and seasons. After saying good

Bamboo poles and wooden cross-country skis were perfect for exploring Forbidden Plateau and Mount Washington.

night to the alpenglow on the glacier, I made a pact to paint one hundred paintings as Georgia O'Keeffe had. The glacier is visible from Fanny Bay to the Oyster River in the Comox Valley. I use different points of view, mediums and themes to create my paintings. Different perspectives trigger my imagination with a myriad of possibilities. I am working on paintings number 44 and 45 now, with new mixtures of blue skies, blue snow, blue fog and clouds, not forgetting to mix in all those yellows and oranges that were so important to Van Gogh.

While Ross draws maps, I paint my vision of the valley. Together we often saunter on Goose Spit and through MacDonald Wood. We are lucky to hike the Beaufort Range mountains, canoe camp on the Sayward chain lakes and boat on the Salish Sea. While Ross throws lures in the ocean or a lake, I paint islands, trees and reflective water. The elements may challenge us, but the Comox Valley and nature hold us. Our children and grandchildren share these special places. Our early days in the Comox Valley inspired us to live our lifelong pursuits and passions. For the last forty years, those passions have brought joy, love, friendship and happiness.

Bob Dylan once said, "The highest purpose of art is to inspire." Volunteering each year at our Vancouver Island Music Festival, I am honoured to be part of the energy and inspiration that brings so much to our valley. While teaching, I am grateful that I have witnessed thousands of students drawing, painting, singing and making music over the years. We left a busy city to live a simpler life, work together to help preserve what we have and honour the chance to be caretakers of our valley. Cherished friends have been part of this amazing environment, finding inspiration in the human and natural richness of the Comox Valley.

Comox Glacier majestically rising,
Beaufort Range rests between the Salish Sea and a blue sky.
With meditating breaths, I become the scene,
A full palette awaits,
My brush draws lines, dabs and begins,
Come join me in the wild blue wonder.

Jane Wilde and high school friend Lenny in 1976, both recently arrived in the Village of Queen Charlotte from urban Southern Ontario, looking for and finding adventure.

Lou Allison at the dock in the Village of Queen Charlotte in 1976, eight months pregnant and counting.

Acknowledgements

First, we wish to thank Monika Terfloth and Sally Gellard for helping Jane pull the writer network together. Warm thanks are due to the Prince Rupert Library, where Lou works, whose technical staff was invaluably helpful and whose management was invariably supportive. Thank you to Sarah Kerr for many of our writers' portraits, to Lia Crowe for Linda Rajotte's portrait, to Jane Gilchrist for the front cover photograph, and to Lynda Glover for the painting on the back cover. To Evelyn Gillespie, owner of the Laughing Oyster Bookshop in Courtenay, thanks for ongoing support and enthusiasm. Thank you to our publishers: Chris Armstrong (Muskeg Press) for taking a chance on *Gumboot Girls* in the first place, and Vici Johnstone (Caitlin Press) for keeping *Gumboot Girls* going and adding this sister volume, *Dancing in Gumboots*.

Finally: a huge thank you to all of the women who shared the stories of their lives throughout the seventies on the north and south coast of BC.

Additional Reading

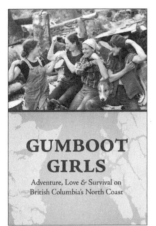

GUMBOOT GIRLS
Adventure, Love & Survival
on the North Coast of British Columbia

Edited by Lou Allison
with Jane Wilde

Forty years ago, droves of young women migrated away from urban settings and settled in rural areas across North America. Many settled on the north coast of British Columbia, on Haida Gwaii or around Prince Rupert. *Gumboot Girls* tells the stories of thirty-four women, through their own eyes, as they moved from their comfortable city-dwelling surroundings to the rugged north coast. Part back-to-the-land, part adventure, heartbreak and love, this collection of stories edited by Lou Allison and compiled by Jane Wilde was inspired by the book *Girls Like Us* by Sheila Weller. Wilde, the creator of *Gumboot Girls*, encouraged, prodded and cajoled her friends (and some of their friends) to tell the story of a generation of young women who flocked to the north coast of BC in the 1970s.